"Martin Tolchin's memoir not only describes a very interesting life but also reminds us of how essential a free press remains for the preservation and advancement of our democracy in a time when our governing authorities are describing the press as 'the enemy of the people,' a phrase reminiscent of what Hitler and Stalin believed."

—**Robert Dallek**, author most recently of
Franklin D. Roosevelt: A Political Life

"This superb memoir traces the evolution of journalism and its impact on politics and history."

—**Bill Kovach**, former Washington
bureau chief of *The New York Times*

"Tolchin's memoir is written with the same clarity and elegance that characterized his news stories. Readers will delight in this opportunity to get to know the person behind the reporting!"

—**Lauren A. Wright**, Princeton University
and author of *Star Power*

"Martin Tolchin is a witness to history, not just as a Washington reporter for *The New York Times* over several decades, but also as a veteran journalist who transitioned from that pinnacle of traditional media to the innovative new media news outlets of *The Hill* and *Politico*. A superb writer with a journalist's keen eye for the details that bring a story to life, Tolchin has created a compelling read of great interest to Political Science and Communication scholars—and their students."

—**Stephen J. Farnsworth**, University of Mary
Washington and author of
Presidential Communication and Character

Media and Power
Series Editor: David L. Paletz

Media and Power is a series that publishes work uniting media studies with studies of power. This innovative and original series features books that challenge, even transcend, conventional disciplinary boundaries, construing both media and power in the broadest possible terms. At the same time, books in the series are designed to fit into several different types of college courses in political science, public policy, communication, journalism, media, history, film, sociology, anthropology, and cultural studies. Intended for the scholarly, text, and trade markets, the series should attract authors and inspire and provoke readers.

Published Books

Age of Oprah
Cultural Icon for the Neoliberal Era
Janice Peck

Mousepads, Shoe Leather, and Hope
Lessons from the Howard Dean Campaign for the Future of Internet Politics
Zephyr Teachout & Thomas Streeter

Politics, Journalism and the Way Things Were
My Life at *The Times*, *The Hill* and *Politico*
Martin Tolchin

www.routledge.com/Media-and-Power/book-series/MP

POLITICS, JOURNALISM AND THE WAY THINGS WERE

In this book, Martin Tolchin describes his journey from *New York Times* copy boy to White House correspondent, and founder of *The Hill* and co-founder of *Politico*. He tells of the talented and eccentric colleagues he encountered en route, and the conflicts and tensions that beset him during his 40-year news career. Along the way, he tracks the evolution of political journalism from mostly all-male, smoke-filled newsrooms to the high-tech world of the 24/7 news cycle. As a local reporter in New York City, Tolchin saw his articles change public policy and re-direct millions of dollars in public funds. Nationally, Tolchin reported on some of the country's most important political leaders, including Ronald Reagan, Jimmy Carter and Tip O'Neill, among many others. As a Washington correspondent he was involved in Iran Contra, the Anita Hill hearings on the nomination of Justice Clarence Thomas and Washington's response to the New York City financial crisis. Mr. Tolchin writes with extraordinary candor and optimism. His story is one that will inform and inspire students, scholars and general readers in an era in which fake news has sometimes overtaken legitimate reporting. He believes in the power of a free press to guard and guide free people.

Martin Tolchin spent 40 years at *The New York Times*, equally divided between New York and Washington. In New York he was City Hall bureau chief and a political and investigative reporter. In Washington he reported on Congress and the White House. He then founded two publications, as editor-in-chief and publisher of *The Hill*, and senior publisher and editor of *Politico*, and served on the jury of the Pulitzer Prizes for Journalism. Mr. Tolchin then was appointed a senior scholar at the Woodrow Wilson International Center for Scholars. Mr. Tolchin was born Sept. 20, 1928, in Brooklyn, N.Y. His father, a furrier, and mother, a housekeeper, were Russian immigrants. He was educated at the Bronx High School of Science, Idaho State College, the University of Utah and New York Law School, where he received an L.L.B. With his wife Susan, a professor of government at George Mason University, he wrote eight books, one of which, *To the Victor: Political Patronage from the Clubhouse to the White House*, has been cited in five U.S. Supreme Court decisions. They had two children, Charles and Karen. Mr. Tolchin lives in Washington, D.C.

POLITICS, JOURNALISM AND THE WAY THINGS WERE

My Life at *The Times, The Hill* and *Politico*

Martin Tolchin

Routledge
Taylor & Francis Group

NEW YORK AND LONDON

First published 2020
by Routledge
52 Vanderbilt Avenue, New York, NY 10017

and by Routledge
2 Park Square, Milton Park, Abingdon, Oxon, OX14 4RN

Routledge is an imprint of the Taylor & Francis Group, an informa business

© 2020 Taylor & Francis

Library of Congress Cataloging-in-Publication Data
A catalog record for this book has been requested

ISBN: 978-0-367-42352-0 (hbk)
ISBN: 978-0-367-36612-4 (pbk)
ISBN: 978-0-367-82373-3 (ebk)

Typeset in Bembo
by Apex CoVantage, LLC

To the memory of Susan, my lifelong partner, who gave me 50 years of love, warmth, wit, intellectuality and just plain fun. And to Karen, Charlie and Barbara, who have brought me much joy.

CONTENTS

Acknowledgments   *xi*

1   The Evolution of Journalism and How
    I Got My Start   1

2   From Idaho State to *The New York Times*   11

3   Finally, I'm a Reporter   21

4   Washington, Here I Come   51

5   A Broader Canvas   63

6   *The Hill* and *Politico*   87

7   Life After Journalism   101

8   A New Day in Journalism   105

Index   *111*

ACKNOWLEDGMENTS

For more than a decade, my daughter Karen has urged me to write a memoir. She thought I had a lot of good stories about the U.S. Congress, which was my beat for 20 years. But I thought, who would be interested in a foot soldier in the army of justice? I never won a Pulitzer (although I was a Pulitzer juror). My top award was the Everett M. Dirksen Award for Distinguished Reporting on Congress. The immediate impetus for this book came from Barbara Rosenfeld, who became my life partner after the death of my beloved Susan, to whom I was married 50 years, and with whom I had written eight books. Barbara is a widow, and we had known each other more than 40 years, traveling together with our spouses. Her husband Steve had been columnist and editor of *The Washington Post*'s editorial page. When Barbara heard some of my stories, and I told her I was thinking of writing a memoir, she figuratively sat me down in front of a computer and told me to write them down, and throw in some analysis as well. What did it all mean?

I had a ball. We all remember things that never were, but I was surprised by my memory, which was enhanced by *The New York Times* archives. I also had the help of *Times* colleagues, including Adam Clymer, Robert Pear, Bill Kovach, Steve Weisman, Barclay Walsh, Matt Wald, Irv Molotsky, Rick Smith, Paul Delaney, Steve Holmes, Steve Labaton, Steve Roberts, Jack Cushman, Bob Hershey, Peter Kilborn, Neil Lewis and Terry Smith. In addition, I was helped by members of my political lunch group, including Jim Lehrer, Mark Shields, Jules Witcover, Roger Mudd, Tom Edsall, Jim Dickenson, Ron Ostrow,

Gerry Slater, Tom Oliphant, Bill Kovach and Jim Doyle. In addition, Bill Kovach and Tom Edsall, along with Karen Tolchin and Barbara Rosenfeld, reviewed the manuscript—to ward off the evil spirits. I also benefited from discussions with colleagues at the Woodrow Wilson International Center for Scholars, where, after my journalistic career, I spent six years as a Senior Scholar. I am especially indebted to the Center's Lee Hamilton, Jane Harman, Mike Van Dusen, Kent Hughes and Don Wolfensberger. John Harris at *Politico*, and Bob Cusack and Sheila Casey at *The Hill* helped me relive my days at those publications. Washington is the epicenter of politics, and friends who cheer and bemoan political developments, and were especially helpful, include Pat Choate, Cokie Roberts, Ken Kesssler, Richard Budson, Bob and Geri Dallek, Mike and Marian Usher, Tom DeMarchi, Joe Perpich, Cathy Sulzberger, Jon Gardner, Kitty Kelley, Alex and Pat Shakow, David and Linda Cashdan, Alan and Irene Wurtzel, John and Barbara Cochran, Richard Ryland and Cathy Wyler. Neil Mulholland offered technical support, as generous with his time as he was awesome with his skills.

I am greatly indebted to my editor, Jennifer Knerr, whose keen eye, creativity, encouragement and support are reflected on every page. This is our third book together.

I'd like to thank the Routledge reviewers, including Stephen J. Farnsworth and Lauren Wright, and series editor David L. Paletz. Also at Routledge, I thank Editorial Assistant Jessica Moran and the production team at Apex CoVantage, all of whom helped to bring this project to fruition.

All those mentioned here have contributed significantly to the creation of this book. Any errors, of course, are my own.

Note: Portions of the final chapter appeared in an essay by Martin Tolchin, "Bigger, Better, Bolder: Some Unconventional Thoughts on the Future of Journalism," *Hinckley Journal of Politics*, Hinckley Institute of Politics, University of Utah, Volume 13, 2012, p. 43, and are reprinted here by permission.

1

THE EVOLUTION OF JOURNALISM AND HOW I GOT MY START

They are quiet now, those smoke–filled newsrooms that used to sparkle with eccentrics and occasionally deafen with the rumble of presses in their basements. No longer does one hear the clatter of typewriters or find bottles of scotch in desk drawers. No longer does one hear the cry of "Copy" or "Boy," when reporters have completed a page of their articles, to send their work to a waiting editor, who would cut and paste their stories.

Newsrooms now look like banks or insurance companies, mostly silent, with low ceilings and cubicles instead of the open spaces of yesteryear. Noiseless computers have replaced the noisy typewriters, and reporters now have college degrees, unlike the many high school dropouts who were among the finest journalists of yesteryear. Nor do today's reporters hang out in bars, rather than take long bus and subway rides to their cramped apartments. In fact, when the passenger ships Andrea Doria and Stockholm collided off the coast of Nantucket in 1956, *The New York Times'* top editors had only to walk across the street to a bar to find all the reporters and editors they needed. Thanks to the Newspaper Guild, most journalists can now afford to rent apartments in town, and buy homes in the suburbs.

These are among the changes ushered in by the digital age, a technological marvel that has both its champions and its critics. Count me among the former. Here's why:

The internet and world wide web have led to a democratization of journalism. One no longer needs a huge physical plant to publish an article that reaches hundreds of thousands of readers. One need not be a millionaire. One only needs a computer. This has led to a proliferation of bloggers, some with large followings. *The New York Times* and other mainstream media organizations have hired some of these bloggers because of their followings and their expertise. This has led to some lively debates about who is and is not a journalist.

Webster's New World Dictionary defines a journalist as one who gathers, writes, edits and disseminates news. Has the prevalence of cell phones made the average person who records a police officer killing an unarmed black man and uploads the video to YouTube a journalist? It's good to know that such abuses, as well as rioters who loot retail stores and other malefactors, may find themselves on the evening news. Do we have to redefine our terms? ·

The internet is merely the latest milestone in the democratization of journalism. Cave drawings were probably the first example of man's efforts to describe his surroundings. Then came papyrus used by the Catholic Church for theological treatises. The printing press, invented in 1450, broke the Church's monopoly on communication, while the telegraph, invented in 1844, allowed for worldwide communication. Then came radio in the early 20th century, followed by television, which allowed viewers to see wars, politicians and major events for themselves. Then came Cable TV, whose hundreds of channels catered to our interests, and biases. Finally came desktop publishing and the internet, which meant you didn't have to be a zillionaire and have a huge physical plant to be a publisher. All you needed was a computer. *The Hill* and *Politico* are among hundreds of desktop publications.

The democratization of journalism was accompanied by a steady increase in literacy, from only priests and aristocrats to the population at large. Knowledge is power. The evolution of journalism has been used for good and ill: The printing press gave wide distribution to both the Bible and *Mein Kampf.* FDR and Hitler were both masters of the radio. Television has fostered extremists on both the left and right. The internet has been used to rally reform movements around the world, as well as to enlist terrorists. President Trump has proven a master at tweets.

Critics have correctly pointed out that unlike reporters who work for the mainstream media, bloggers have no fact checkers or gatekeepers. It is also true, however, that major media organizations sometimes used gatekeepers to feather their own nests, including supporting political candidates who gave them favors. In *The Power Broker*, Robert Caro described how the Manhattan entrance to the Triboro Bridge was moved from 96th Street to 125th Street to accommodate William Randolph Hearst, who owned a great deal of real estate above 96th Street. Hearst reciprocated by banning all newspaper criticism of Robert Moses, the official responsible for this change, and the subject of Caro's book. The internet also has led to the demise of many fine mainstream publications, and a severe reduction in revenue for most of the rest.

The media and politicians have always been at cross-purposes, but President Trump has brought this enmity to new heights. Labeling reporters "the enemies of the people," and demeaning individual newspapers such as "the failing *New York Times*," Trump maintains that the mass media specializes in fake news. Never mind that he has told more than 10,000 lies in his first 2 ½ years in office, according to *The Washington Post*. One example: Trump denounced as "fake news" *The New York Times* article asserting that the president asked Matthew Whitaker, then acting Attorney General, to have an ally oversee the investigation of payoffs to two women with whom Trump allegedly had affairs. The ally, Geoffrey Berman, U.S. Attorney in the Southern District of New York, had recused himself from the investigation. The president offered no specifics on what exactly was wrong with *The Times'* article. (*New York Times*, Feb. 20, 2019, p. 1).

Unfortunately for Trump, *The Times, The Post, The Wall Street Journal* and other mass media publications have had banner years reporting on his administration, reaping multiple awards in the process. Trump also has been good for business. Readership, radio news listenership and TV news viewers have markedly increased, despite their earlier decline because of the loss of advertising caused by the internet. Editors caution reporters not to respond to Trump's vitriol but to do the best journalism they can do. They have exposed his lies, financial blustering, Russian ties, alienation of allies, pettiness and mean-spirited actions, among other failings.

A.G. Sulzberger, publisher of *The Times*, lambasted President Trump's threats against journalists in an off-the-record Oval Office meeting with the president July 20, 2019. "I told the president directly that I thought his language was not just divisive but increasingly dangerous," the 37-year-old publisher said. "I told him that although the phrase 'fake news' is untrue and harmful, I am far more concerned about his labeling journalists 'the enemy of the people,'" he continued. "I warned that his inflammatory language is contributing to a rise in threats against journalists and will lead to violence," especially overseas, where dictators are emboldened by Trump's attacks on the media. They were "putting lives at risk," and "undermining the democratic ideals of our nation," Mr. Sulzberger said.

He felt entitled to break the "off-the-record" restriction after the president said in a Tweet that he and Mr. Sulzberger had discussed "the vast amounts of Fake News being put out by the media and how that Fake News had morphed into the phrase, 'Enemy of the People.' Sad!" (ibid)

What follows is the story of my own particular journalistic evolution, from the lowliest position—copy boy at *The New York Times*—all the way to White House correspondent in its Washington bureau and then on to the founding of *The Hill* and *Politico*. Along the way are some side trips into how journalism has changed, and along with it, politics and our perceptions of it, as citizens and people in the world.

★★★

On March 5, 1953, when I was 24, I thought my life was over. I was on a train from Ft. Meade, Md., to Penn Station, N.Y., having just received my Army discharge. It was not the usual "Honorable Discharge," but a "General Discharge," given "for the good of the service."

The reason: As a teenager and young adult, I had belonged to several groups that the U.S. Attorney General designated "subversive." These included the Book Find Club, which advertised in *The New York Times*, and I joined to get two books: John Roy Carlson's *Under Cover*, which described his penetration of right-wing extremist groups, and Ray Josephs' *Argentine Diary*, which described his life as Buenos Aires correspondent for the United Press. Josephs eventually became a successful public relations man for whom I worked during the fabled New York 113-day newspaper strike. A short, elegant workaholic with wavy white hair, Joseph asked me to stay on after the strike was settled, at twice the salary I had been receiving as a journalist. But I enjoyed being a newspaper reporter and turned him down.

In high school I also briefly joined a Marxist study group, had some left-wing political pamphlets including one by the actress Katherine Hepburn that began, "I speak because I am an American," and attended a Pete Seeger concert. These were the activities that marked me as a "subversive" in the eyes of the U.S. Army. These facts probably came to the Army's attention through someone I had befriended when I worked as a stock clerk at Macy's on Thursday nights and all day Saturday, to help pay for law school. Who knew that his father was head of the New York City's police department's anti-subversive unit? One night I invited him to dinner, and he borrowed the pamphlets.

The Army charges against me also included allegations against my mother, a housewife with a keen eye for injustice. As a teenager, she had worked at a sewing machine in a sweat shop in New York's Garment Center, but managed to get a high school diploma in night school. She was one of the best-read people I ever knew, devouring everything from romantic fiction to books on politics and international affairs. She also loved the theater. Her pocketbook was filled with newspaper clippings, which she would retrieve to score points in political arguments. I knew she was politically left, went to demonstrations to protest lynching, campaigned for voting rights for blacks and would never cross a union picket line. She believed that if people felt strongly enough to strike and forfeit their salaries, that was good enough for her. My parents and I would sometimes approach a theater showing a movie we wanted to see, but if the theater had a picket line, we went home. I've always felt the same way, with one notable exception: a *New York Times* strike by printers who sought to continue featherbedding, getting paid for work not done. But like most members of the Newspaper Guild, I didn't cross the printers' picket line. After their strike was settled, and the Guild went on strike, the printers happily crossed our picket line. So much for "solidarity forever." In any event, my father, a political moderate who often voted Republican, couldn't have cared less about my mother's political views and activities. A furrier, he had little respect for the furriers' union, which he regarded as corrupt and whose president ended up in prison. He had suffered from diabetes and ulcers, and died of a heart attack at the age of 51, when I was 14.

Despite my law degree, I feared that this "less than honorable" Army discharge would make it impossible for me to be admitted to the bar. I was right. Because I was drafted between the time I received my law degree and the next bar exam, the state waived the exam, but I had one more hurdle, the Committee on Character and Fitness. When I eventually faced a panel of five lawyers in the gilded courtroom of the Appellate Division of New York's Supreme Court in Manhattan, I was told that if I wanted admission to the bar I had to identify my friends, especially my high school friends in the Marxist study group. I declined, not wanting to put them through the same hell I was going through. So, three years of law school went down the drain. It was three years of my life, thousands of dollars and thousands of hours of study. I thought I would have made a good lawyer, too. In retrospect, I think I had a much more exciting and fulfilling life in journalism, but nothing could have been further from my mind during that train ride.

I feared that it would be impossible for me to find any meaningful employment. How could I support myself and the family I hoped to have? As the train sped past farms and towns, I wondered what I'd tell my family and friends, who knew my military discharge date was scheduled for six months later.

This is the story of how, despite this devastating experience, I landed a copy boy's job at *The New York Times*, earning $41.50 a week and living on New York's west side in a single room occupancy building, with a bathroom down the hall. I spent 40 years at *The Times*, in both New York and Washington, reported on New York politics, the White House and Congress, and then founded *The Hill* newspaper and helped found *Politico*. My top salary and bonuses as a journalist exceeded $300,000 a year. I also received income from *The New York Times* stock options, which put my kids through college, and the eight books I had written with my wife (one of which has been cited in five decisions of the U.S. Supreme Court), as well as lecture fees that were spinoffs of those books. I also won several awards, and did a stint as a Pulitzer jurist.

Like many of my journalistic colleagues, I saw my articles change public policy, and re-direct tens of millions of dollars in government funds. My primary concern was the plight of the poor, sick, elderly and disinherited. I sought to follow the journalistic credo, "Comfort the afflicted and afflict the comfortable." In this effort, the owners of *The Times*, *The Hill* and *Politico* gave me unstinting support.

But my efforts paled compared to the media's reporting of the Vietnam War, refuting the rosy estimates made by President Lyndon Johnson and Defense Secretary Robert McNamara, which was critical in ending public support for the war and bringing the war to an end. My *Times* colleagues David Halberstam and Neil Sheehan played a key role with their reporting. When President Kennedy sought to have Halberstam reassigned, *Times* publisher Punch Sulzberger extended his tour.

Similarly, my *Times* colleague David Burnham almost singlehandedly fought corruption in the New York City police department. His articles led to a significant reduction in corruption among top police officers. But the payoffs to police officers from the mafia, drug dealers and other miscreants were so pervasive, so much a part of police culture, that its total elimination was impossible.

In this day and age, it's hard to appreciate the intensity of the national frenzy, in the late 1940s and early 1950s, against not just communists but also "fellow travelers," meaning anyone who agreed with communists on any issue. Although a lowly 24-year-old PFC, I was caught up in a national fever. The Soviets had just exploded an atom bomb, and the McCarthyites thought this could not have happened without the help of two American communists: Julius and Ethel Rosenberg, who were executed. Half a century later, Ethel's brother, David Greenglass, admitted that it was his wife, not Ethel, who was complicit in the crime, taking notes on a family typewriter about construction of an atomic bomb. His testimony had led to Ethel's conviction and execution. Greenglass told Sam Roberts of *The New York Times* that he had lied on the witness stand to save his wife (*The Brother: The Untold Story of Atomic Spy David Greenglass and How*

He Sent His Sister, Ethel Rosenberg, to the Electric Chair, by Sam Roberts, Random House, 2001).

Alger Hiss added fuel to the fire. He was a perfect foil, a patrician with an Ivy League education who worked in the State Department and was at FDR's side at international conferences. He also spied for the Soviets. It was the heyday of McCarthyism. To counter Republican accusations that the Democrats had fostered "twenty years of treason," President Harry Truman initiated a Loyalty Oath and the U.S. Attorney General created a list of "subversive" organizations. Adopted by states and localities, as well as many businesses including the film industry, the Loyalty Oath cost the jobs of grade school teachers and college professors, accountants, janitors, actors, directors, screen writers, scientists, maintenance workers and those on every step of the ladder in the labor force. In his memoir, Clark Clifford, a top Truman aide, wrote that the Loyalty Oath was the action that Truman most regretted (*Counsel to the President: A Memoir* by Clark Clifford, Random House, 1991).

At Ft. Meade, a kindly Warrant Officer, Mr. Shaeffer, tried to soften the blow of my less than honorable discharge. His long experience in the military had taught him how to make a slight tear in the accompanying discharge papers, so that the word "general" did not appear before the word "discharge." But there it was, on my actual discharge diploma, big as life.

A few years later, an outraged Supreme Court, in a unanimous decision, struck down the Army's policy of giving general discharges on the basis, not of military misconduct, but "political" activities and associations prior to induction. I now have an honorable discharge and accompanying discharge papers, which rest in my safe deposit box. Similarly, the New York bar stopped inquiring into the political associations of its applicants. And in 1954, Senator McCarthy was censured by the Senate, and his crusade against "subversives" discredited. But not before tens of thousands had lost their jobs and been otherwise injured by his tactics.

Some may read this and say, "I always knew that *The Times* was a commie-pinko rag," but I've always considered it a daily miracle, with reporting in depth from around the globe and on virtually every subject—from finance to sex. Sadly, *The Times* also was caught up in the hysteria of the moment, and dismissed those who invoked the

Fifth Amendment before House and Senate committees investigating their beliefs.

A quarter century later, my Army discharge continued to haunt me. When *The Times* assigned me to the White House, I had to be cleared by the Secret Service. Would I lose my job? My best friend William Safire advised me to inform *The Times'* top editors of my initial discharge and being rejected by the bar committee. I raised the issue when A.M. Rosenthal, then *The Times'* managing editor, and Arthur Gelb, his deputy, paid a visit to the Washington bureau. They laughed it off, saying the McCarthy era was long gone, and good riddance. I heaved a huge sigh of relief. No matter what the Secret Service did, I would keep my job. Thankfully, I received my Secret Service accreditation without incident, and reported on Jimmy Carter's White House.

But of course I did not start with the White House assignment; a circuitous, and often fortuitous, path led me there. Almost from the very beginning, however, I encountered people and events that would point me in that direction.

I met Safire shortly after my father's death, when my mother and I moved to an apartment hotel, the Windermere, on West End Avenue and 92nd Street. Bill's father, Oscar, a textile manufacturer with factories in the south, also had died, and Bill's mother, Ida, moved the family into the Windermere for the same reason my mother moved us there: daily housekeeping, room service and a very good restaurant, where Bill and I would sometimes dine together when our mothers stayed out late. Like me, Bill also had passed the Bronx Science entrance exam, and we traveled to school together, taking the 96th St. crosstown bus to Central Park West, where we picked up the D train to the Bronx. We both struggled at the school, and did much of our homework on the 45-minute trip each way.

Bronx Science was a tough slog. I knew I was in trouble my first day, when most students arrived wearing a foot-long wooden slab attached to their belts. I had never even seen a slide rule, much less knew how to use one. My first report card showed I was failing every major subject, including English and History, my favorite subjects. After my father's death, I found it difficult to concentrate in school, or even listen to my teachers. Fortunately, I pulled out of my slump to get all passing grades, but not much better. I was called into a school counselor's office and told if my grades didn't improve, I would flunk out of Science. Students were required to take three years of math, including calculus, and four years of science, including physics. I had always been a word guy who also loved history and current events, not a math or science guy. Along with my new friend, William Safire, I struggled mightily, always just one step away from expulsion. Miraculously, I graduated with an 86 average, but this put me near the bottom of my class. At Science, a 92 average put you in the bottom half of the class.

Even in those days, Bill Safire and I were interested in politics. Bill was a conservative, and I was a liberal. But on election days, we would distribute the buttons and literature of any candidate who gave them to us, Republican or Democrat, liberal or conservative. We didn't care. Our best customers were the ladies of the evening who worked in a brothel across 92nd street from the Windermere. Bill wrote a column about it when I was *The New York Times* convention coordinator in 1992 and the Democrats convened at Madison Square Garden. Bill always had an open mind. He recalled that, while we were both in high school, I took him to his first (and only) Vito Marcantonio rally. For many years, Representative Marcantonio represented Spanish Harlem. He was very far left, a firebrand.

I graduated from Bronx Science by the skin of my teeth. My college advisor said, "We'll start in Colorado and work our way west." That's how I ended up at the University of Utah, in Salt Lake City, after a short stint at Idaho State College, in Pocatello.

2

FROM IDAHO STATE TO
THE NEW YORK TIMES

I was thrilled with my sojourn in the intermountain west, briefly at Idaho State and then the University of Utah. I loved the scenery and especially the people. It gave me a whole new perspective on life. In New York, people were your natural enemy: you rushed to beat old ladies to a seat in the subway. Traffic jams were the norm, and restaurant reservations hard to come by. But in the intermountain west, where you can go days without seeing a human being, people are highly valued. There's a lot more cooperation than competition. The old saying that people get nicer as you go farther west, until California, is true. I received a deferment from military service until my law school graduation.

The train trip to Idaho took three nights and nearly four days. I took the New York Central overnight to Chicago and the Union Pacific to Pocatello Idaho, a train junction in the heart of a rural community not far from Salt Lake City. It was September 1946. Most state universities, begging for students during the war years, were now overrun with returning veterans and not accepting out-of-state students. On the train I befriended a couple of veterans, and we shared a motel room when we first arrived in Pocatello. Many of my classes were in Quonset huts because there were not enough classrooms to accommodate the large student body. Idaho State also had a shortage of dorm rooms, but eventually we all found lodging on campus. Because of its proximity to Salt Lake City, most students were Mormons. Many of the Mormon girls considered a New York Jew an exotic creature, but their religion forbade anything approaching intimacy. Of course, those who had left the church had a somewhat different perspective.

Freshman hazing came three weeks after we arrived. The veterans, of course, wouldn't put up with any of that nonsense, but the rest of us were subjected to a day of rattlesnake hunting. The slag hills surrounding the college were full of rattlers. We didn't know that most of them were beginning to hibernate (the snakes, not the sophomores). We nevertheless found enough to fill a burlap bag. I soon joined the staff of the *Idaho State Bengal*, the school newspaper, covering sports, and in my first and only year at Idaho State, became sports editor. I enjoyed the camaraderie of the athletes, especially the football players. My courses were a breeze after Bronx Science, and without any effort I was a gentleman-C student.

With the help of the Rev. Ed Cunningham, a Congregational minister, I started a club called "The Seeker's Club." Ed was a modest, outgoing ethics professor at the college. We had a one-hour radio show on a local station, broadcast from the college, and invited various politicians, authors and faculty members to join us in our search for truth. Subjects ranged from local and national issues to the proper role of citizens in various moral dilemmas.

My best friend was Richard (Pete) Bradley, from nearby Twin Falls. Pete was a blunt, no-nonsense guy who was a good athlete. I would go home with him some weekends, and he taught me how to hunt and fish. Our first time out, we got up before dawn, went out in his pickup truck and found a deer caught in our headlights. Although it's considered unsporting to shoot a deer in that situation, Pete had no qualms. He wanted to relieve his dad's pressure to come home with a trophy. Pete and I also spent a spring weekend at Sun Valley, where we stayed in a dorm and enjoyed ice skating.

That June, Pete and I were accepted by the University of Utah, a large, cosmopolitan university that then had 1,000 foreign students and a considerable Jewish population. The Mormons considered themselves one of the lost tribes of Israel and had great respect for Jews, whom they elected to everything from governor to sheriff. The

Mormons favored Brigham Young University, in nearby Provo. But there was a considerable Mormon population at the U, and coeds would come into my room, fall on their knees and pray for my salvation.

The university offered a combined undergraduate and law degree that appealed to me. I also joined the daily newspaper, *The Chronicle*, and contributed to the literary magazine. I soon discovered a group of left-wing easterners, whom I eagerly joined. As in such previous encounters, I was largely attracted by the women, and I had a year-long relationship with one of them. She introduced me to sex. It happened in a cemetery, since there seemed to be no other place we could have privacy. Afterward I discovered that I had lost my wallet as well as my virginity. The wallet had fallen out of my pocket, and I went back in the total darkness to find the tombstone near where we had frolicked. It took a while, but I eventually found my wallet and raced back to my room. The young woman went on to have a distinguished academic career and we meet for lunch every summer in Vermont to catch up with each other.

It was 1948, and we were all involved in Students for Wallace—Former Vice President Henry A. Wallace. President Truman seemed too establishment for us, and Thomas E. Dewey, the Republican, was out of the question. Wallace's running mate was Glenn Taylor, a singing cowboy who became a U.S. senator from nearby Idaho. Taylor came to visit us one day and was so patronizing that I lost all interest in the campaign.

Despite my new leftish friends, I discovered I had an entrepreneurial spirit. Since my dad had been a furrier, I decided to manufacture fur bowties, which I called, in a burst of creativity, Furbows. I ordered the pelts from a furrier in Chicago. I was then living in a rooming house and had the lady of the house and her friends cut the pelts and attach clips, for clip-ons. I advertised on a local radio show hosted by Al (Jazzbo) Collins, and persuaded a downtown Salt Lake City department store, Zion's Cooperative Mercantile Institution, to buy them on consignment. One morning at a bus stop, wearing my Furbow, I encountered a woman who told me that she had had a terrible argument with her husband, who had purchased a Furbow, to her dismay.

For the first time in a long time, I was engrossed by my academic subjects, especially law school. Constitutional law was my favorite class. My grades improved markedly. But in my second year we studied water rights and cattle disputes, and since I planned to practice law in Manhattan, where there are few such disputes, I knew I had to go back East.

Returning to New York, I applied for admission to Columbia Law School and the New York University law school, but they would not give me credit for my two years at the University of Utah law school. However, New York Law School gave me full credit and an L.L.B. in June 1951.

I received my law degree in the middle of the Korean War. I had received deferments to attend college and law school, but they finally had run out. The bar exam was held in October, but I was drafted into the Army in September. Since I had not taken the bar exam, I was not a lawyer, and entered the service as a dogface Private E-2, eventually rising to Private First Class.

I did my basic training with a group of Kentuckians at Indiantown Gap, near Harrisburg, Pa. Since I was 23 and most of them were still in their late teens, they sometimes called me "the old man." The camp was located in a gap in the Shenandoah mountains, and when the weather turned cold the wind whistled through that gap. On bivouacs, some of my buddies' toes were frozen and had to be amputated.

Training with the Kentuckians was a challenge. Unlike me, they were completely familiar with rifles, which terrified me, while they could assemble one blindfolded. They also had no trouble with heights and could maneuver an obstacle course with ease. At the end of my training I got the measles and was hospitalized for several days. This was fortunate, since my company was sent to Korea. I completed basic training with another company and was sent to Ft. Bliss, Texas, for artillery training. It was January, and I was glad to escape both the cold of Indiantown Gap and the risks to life and limb in Korea. I was eventually assigned a company housed on the Maryland shore and spent my days handing artillery shells to gunners. I decided to see the adjutant, a major. "Do you have permission from your company commander to talk to me?" he asked. "No sir," I replied. "Do you have permission from your first sergeant?" No sir,"

I said. "Well go ahead, son, what's on your mind?" he said. I told him that since I had gone to college and had a law degree, and moreover was an excellent typist, perhaps I could better serve the Army as a company clerk. A few days later, that's the job I got at a company located at Ft. Meade, Md.

It sure beat handling shells. But one of the sergeants took an instant dislike to me. He had served in Korea and considered me a slacker who enjoyed a premier job without ever having seen combat. He gave me letters to type, always omitting a key directive, so that I had to rewrite a single letter many times. He then suggested that we go outside and settle our differences. Since my fisticuff skills were even worse than my military skills, I demurred. "You're afraid to hit a sergeant?" he said. "Don't worry. I'll take off my stripes." No way, I said. One day I received a notice to report to the commanding general. He had seen that I had gone to college and law school and wanted to send me to Ft. Benjamin Harrison in Indianapolis to become his private secretary. He also would promote me to sergeant, he said. But I would have to serve an additional two years in the Army. I turned him down.

One weekend, on leave but in uniform, I dropped into Patelson's Music store, on 56th Street, to pick up some sheet music and the score of a Broadway musical. I enjoyed playing the piano and having my friends sing along with me. The store was across the street from Carnegie Hall's stage door, and when my date and I left, we saw that the stage door was open. We walked in and saw there was a piano on the stage, illuminated by a single standing lamp. The hall itself was pitch black. I sat down at the piano and began playing show tunes. The maintenance men lit the hall, tier by tier, first the orchestra, then the dress circle and balconies. When I finished playing, they applauded. I think it was my uniform that prompted their kindness, but the fact is I've played Carnegie Hall.

When I returned to my base, something amazing happened. The company got general court martial jurisdiction, and the Jag Officer, Lt. Col Peter Manson, a southerner whom the Army had sent to Emory University law school, became our JAG. He looked down the list of those in the company, saw I had a law degree and invited me to work with him on special and general court martials. What a break. I immediately accepted. I loved the work, but our barracks was located about five miles from 2d Army HQ, and his office. Being a New Yorker, I had never learned to drive and had no driver's license. The Army gave me a car and driver—the sergeant who had taunted me. He drove me to work and drove me home. Sometimes I was in the middle of a case when he came to drive me home, and I told him to either wait or return. This did nothing to improve our relationship. When I received the charges against both me and my mother, Col. Manson and several other senior officers wrote letters attesting to my patriotism, but to no avail.

My re-entry into civilian life was marked by questions from my friends and family. How did I get out six months before my discharge date? I told my closest relatives and friends. I changed the subject for everyone else. Because I was drafted before I could take the bar exam, I was in a special category in which the bar exam was waived. My only obstacle was the Committee on Character and Fitness. Waiting for a session with the committee, I got a job with a law firm, Lesser & Lesser. The younger brother was called the lesser of the two Lessers. After a few months, a friend got me a job with Liberty Mutual Liability Insurance Company. My job was scheduling examinations before trial, many of which were cancelled at the last minute, leaving me to absorb the wrath of outraged lawyers. A few months later, as previously noted, I flunked my session with the Character Committee. What to do?

I received an invitation from the Veterans Administration to attend a two-day course called "How to Get a Job." It was held in the auditorium of Washington Irving High School in Manhattan. The auditorium was packed with more than 500 veterans. The course was taught by a direct mail advertising executive named McDonald. He began by saying that this was the beginning of our real lives, and the most important decision we had to make was "What is it you enjoy doing?" If you work at something you enjoy doing, he said, you won't resent the scut work, long hours and petty humiliations that come with an every job. Once we made that decision, he said, we should write to no fewer than 100 CEOs of companies that employ folks who do what we'd like to do. One could get their names from industry directories. Under no circumstances write to a company's personnel or human relations executives. The letter should be brief, say that you've always admired their product, and you'd be honored to work for the company in any position, as long as there was an opportunity for advancement. The last paragraph should ask, "May I call your office Tuesday morning (or whenever) to ask for an appointment?" The reason: to keep control of the process. "Initiate, don't respond," was McDonald's clarion call. I wrote to 110 newspaper executive editors and managing editors, along with top editors of publishing houses and a few advertising agencies. The letters, written individually, before photocopiers, resulted in six interviews and four job offers. As a veteran with a law degree, I thought I was qualified to be a reporter or advertising copywriter. Instead, I was offered jobs as copy boy with *The New York Times*, *The New York Post* and *The New York Daily News*, and mail room boy at a Chicago advertising agency. McDonald said that the first job should be regarded as a foot in the door. One should make oneself useful to those doing the job you really wanted, and they would help you get it. I took the job with *The Times*, which I had read and revered since childhood. *The Times* didn't want to see the discharge diploma but rather the discharge paper, which Mr. Schaeffer had doctored.

When I first walked into *The Times*' newsroom, I was awestruck. There were some of the greatest reporters of their time, including Meyer Berger, who danced on his desk and whistled in late afternoons; Harrison Salisbury, who wrote "The 900 Days," about the siege of St. Petersburg; Homer Bigart, winner of two Pulitzer Prizes; and Murray Shumach, who had made his reputation covering the Korean War. Some aspects of the newsroom were surprising. There were always a couple of bridge or poker games in the afternoon, and many reporters kept small whisky bottles in their desks. Those days are gone forever. Then again, copy editors used copy paper as handkerchiefs, then tossed them on the floor.

What did a copy boy do (there were no copy girls)? He ran errands, filled pastepots (in the pre-digital age) and answered when a reporter yelled "copy," indicating he had completed a page of his article and wanted to send it to the copy desk. Demeaning for a 25-year-old veteran with a law degree? Actually, every *New York Times* copy boy had a graduate degree, mostly Master's degrees, and a few PhDs. We were told that if we were not promoted within a year we were expected to resign. Promotions were based on the number and quality of articles we got into the paper, mostly in the Metro section and special sections including Travel and Automobiles. Most of us spent our days off wandering the streets, going into churches, synagogues, police precincts, laundries and other retail shops, and asking, "What's everybody so upset about in this neighborhood?" There was always an issue of great concern to the residents, resulting in Metro desk stories.

I was accompanied on my forays by a group I met playing four-wall handball at the 92nd Street Y. They had formed a social club that I joined. We walked the city, meeting at the Museum of Modern Art on Saturdays at noon. I also revived a Y newspaper, the *Y Bulletin*, a weekly to which they contributed. They were a group of amiable eccentrics. Paul the Miser's family owned a delicatessen on the Lower East Side. All the family members except Paul took their turns in the kitchen and at the counter. Paul, a somewhat rotund, good natured young man, found he couldn't work the cash register because his hands broke out in a rash whenever he touched quarters, nickels, dimes and pennies. A confirmed bachelor, he rarely dated, and when he did we would always ask him if it was serious. His response: "I should spend my life supporting a stranger?" He never did.

Morris, another member of the group, wrote mysteries, westerns, science fiction and porn. He was the oldest member of the group, and his hair was prematurely gray. He would walk the city, looking for story ideas, and had won an Edgar (Allen Poe) from the Mystery Writers of America for *Guilty Witness*, the best mystery short story of the year. Morris dedicated a book, *Sex for Three* to me, but Morris himself used a pen name, Arnold English. When I asked him why my name was on the book and his wasn't, Morris cheerfully explained, "I should put my name on a book like that?" From time to time friends have told me that they were in a bookstore and noticed I had a book dedicated to me. I always asked what they were doing in that kind of bookstore. Although a confirmed bachelor in his late 30s, Morris took up with his porno editor, whom he called "Mrs. Brown," shortly after his mother died. He called me one day and said they were going to get married, and I instantly offered our home in Montclair, N.J., for his wedding reception. It occurred on Buzz Aldrin Day, as Montclair paid tribute to the astronaut, a native son. Our house was across the street from the high school football field, where the governor landed in a helicopter and six marching bands helped celebrate the occasion. Recalling Neil Armstrong's famous line when he set foot on the moon, "One small step for man, one giant leap for mankind," we put a sign on our front door, "One small step for Buzz Aldrin, one giant leap for Morris Hershman."

Victor had a gravelly voice and the best sense of humor in the group. He worked in a probation office, initially writing probation reports that he said no one read. He and his office colleagues then gave those reports minimal attention, focusing instead on the annual reports of corporations. They created their own mutual fund, working out of a probation office that had piles of annual reports, and made a great deal of money. When one of us was seriously ill, Victor announced that he "wanted to check in before Jack checks out." Jack was a holocaust survivor who worked as a social worker.

Sam, tall, thin and lacking in self-confidence, was a public relations man who had a long affair with a stunningly beautiful French woman. He had been raised in a Jewish orphanage, returning every so often to tell the children that better times were ahead. Jack and Ray were holocaust survivors who had been children in Nazi concentration camps. Ray labored years writing a book called *And Then Came the Spring*. It never was published. Jack was a psychiatric social worker. I enlisted all of them to write for the *Y Bulletin*, and Morris was the most prolific. He wrote a weekly column called "Heroes of Science." His first hero: Agamemnon Rubberband, the man who invented the rubberband.

Copy boys freelanced the entire paper, and one of us, Jerry Landauer, wrote freelance editorials. He started small, with editorials on innocuous subjects like the flower of the month, and ended writing major editorials on national security. I was amazed that *The Times* published a copy boy's opinions on these major issues. Jerry ended up as a star *Wall Street Journal* reporter.

The head copy boy was a short, middle-aged man, Angelo Gheraldi, who also was *The Times* "bookie." He serviced the newsroom, starting with the managing editor, the reporters and copy editors, photographers and even the copy boys. The police raided *The Times* newsroom periodically, certain that there was bookmaking, but unable to locate the source. He hid when the lobby attendant called the newsroom to warn that the police were on the way up.

It took me nine months to get my first promotion, to news clerk, a glorified copy boy who compiled lists and reported on Sunday morning church sermons. I was assigned to every major church, including St. Patrick's Cathedral, St. John the Divine and Heavenly Rest, and was thrilled to see my 400-word articles in Monday's newspaper. It took another nine months to get promoted to news assistant at the United Nations bureau, which was comprised of journalists who had covered World War II. The bureau chief was Thomas Jefferson Hamilton Jr., a southerner who initially wanted someone else for the job but later gave me a great report. Others in the bureau included Lindsay Parrott, whose wife Ursula was a best-selling author; Kathleen Teltsch, who had an artificial arm and typed rapidly with the fingers of her good hand; and Kathleen McLaughlin, a beautiful woman. Lindsay Parrott and Kathleen Teltsch hated each other and once, in a drunken state, Lindsay threw his typewriter at Kathleen. It landed at the end of his desk. I was deputized to play chess with Lindsay during the late afternoon hours, to keep him occupied when everyone else was churning out copy. The bureau was very generous to me, allowing me to cover press conferences, and helping shape my stories. On that basis, after three years at *The Times*, I finally was promoted to reporter.

3

FINALLY, I'M A REPORTER

Because I had been fairly successful getting stories into the paper, I was asked by Richard Burritt, an assistant managing editor in charge of newsroom personnel, if I was interested in covering family life on the Women's Page, which then reported on fashions, furnishings and food, in addition to family—the so-called Four Fs. I jumped at the chance to be a reporter. It was a three-person department, just me, the editor, Dorothy Barclay, and a secretary named Phyllis whose husband was an executive at the B. Altman department store. Dorothy was a kindly woman in her mid-40s, who would turn my unsophisticated copy into respectable articles.

Early on, I was sent to Washington to report on a National Institute of Health conference on children's mental illnesses. The keynote speaker was a famous psychiatrist, Fritz Redl, director of an NIH project that led to his book, *Children Who Hate*. I arrived late, and they were out of programs. I had never heard of Redl and was too embarrassed to ask how he spelled his name. In my article, I misspelled it the way it was pronounced, Raydel. Dorothy quietly corrected this most grievous mistake without saying a word to me. I learned of the correction when I read the article in the paper. I learned a powerful lesson: there are no stupid questions, only stupid answers.

Reporting is a balancing act: you have to be close enough to politicians to have them confide in you, but not so close that you carry their water. Some of the best reporters maintain a façade of naivete. In fact, one of *The Times*' greatest reporters, Homer Bigart, intentionally presented himself as a bumpkin. News sources felt comfortable talking to him, sometimes to their regret, for he often obtained information that no one else could get and public officials were anxious to conceal. Homer won two Pulitzer Prizes.

There's no substitute for shoe leather in developing a story. Face-to-face meetings are essential. I learned early on to let the interviewee do all the talking. If an interviewee hesitates to search for a word, don't supply it for him. It may not be what he was groping for, and that completely set the interviewee off on another track. It's okay to sit in silence for a few minutes. In writing profiles, I would tell my reporters that if they did all the research they could do and interviewed all the people they could think of, and then interviewed the person they were profiling, and didn't change their perceptions of him, they never really met him. Everyone is different from public perceptions of him or her. Examining public records also is essential. Many great stories lurk behind columns of figures.

There were definite advantages in working for the Women's Page. Since I only wrote features, I never had to worry about deadlines. I found the subject of family life intensely interesting. And there were some great people on the page, including Craig Claiborne, the slim food critic with whom I often had lunch—he preferred sawdust-on-the-floor bars, since he spent his evenings at four-star restaurants including Lutece and Le Bernadin. Paddy's Clam House was one of our favorites. George O'Brien, the furnishings editor, also was a pal. Charlotte Curtis, whose candid articles later revolutionized coverage of society news; Nan Robertson, who went on to win a Pulitzer Prize; Gloria Emerson, who had covered the Vietnam War; Marylin Bender, Carrie Donovan and eventually Dorothy Barclay became good friends. It was an all-star team.

Nan's Pulitzer resulted from an article assigned by Abe Rosenthal, *The Times*' executive editor, when Nan was depressed while recovering from Toxic Shock Syndrome, which led to the amputation of the tips of every finger except her thumbs. He called her when she was still in the hospital and gave her the assignment, which she said she couldn't possibly do. Abe persisted and prevailed, as usual. Who said he had no heart? Her first-person account, "Toxic Shock," appeared in the *Sunday Magazine* on Sept. 19, 1982.

Earlier, she was a leading figure in *The Times'* women's lawsuit for pay equality, which resulted in a lump sum payment of $350,000 and *The Times'* promise of an affirmative action program for women. She ultimately wrote a book about the plight of *Times* women and the ensuing lawsuit, *The Girls in the Balcony: Women, Men and* The New York Times. The title referred to the fact that at that time, the National Press Club was off limits to women reporters. Not only were women denied membership, but during news conferences, important speeches and other events held at the club, while the men dined on the main floor of the club's ballroom, the foodless women were relegated to the balcony. Nan's book was very kind to me, noting my support of *Times* women.

The editor of the Women's Page was Elizabeth Penrose Howkins, a Brit in her mid-50s, whom *The Times* had lured from her position as editor of *British Vogue*—or Vo-Gew as she pronounced it. Of the four Fs, her main interest was fashion, while family rated not at all in her eyes. Her husband was a major in the British army who had long served in India. She held weekly staff meetings, during which she invariably picked on one of her reporters. Sometimes the women fled the meeting in tears. I knew it was just a matter of time until she found fault with me. Finally it was my turn. I was wearing black slacks, a dark blue shirt and a brown sports jacket. "Marty, that outfit you're wearing looks very garment center," she said, making "garment center" sound déclassé. "I come by it honestly, Mrs. Howkins," I said. "My father worked in the garment center. He was a furrier." She looked mortified.

When I wrote an article on marriages between people in their 80s and 90s, she called me into her office. She took issue with a sentence that said that geriatricians observed that sex was often a factor in these marriages. "That's ridiculous," she said. "I'm going to read this to Dr. Goldstein." David Goldstein was *The Times'* house physician. As I sat in her office, I heard her end of the telephone conversation. "It is?" she asked. "They do?" She acted like a little girl who had just discovered that the entire world except her celebrated Christmas.

I decided to improve our relationship. I knew the secret was never to show fear. So one day in mid-morning, when she was reading her mail, I walked into her office, described a play I had seen the night before and sat on a corner of her desk while she responded. Then I walked out. I did this several times, until she said at a staff meeting, "I don't know what's happened to Marty. He's become a terrific asset."

Dorothy also wrote a weekly column in the Sunday magazine, called "Parent & Child." When she left *The Times* to marry a Chicago journalist with many children, I inherited the column. I was then in my early 30s, unmarried and with no children. I knew absolutely nothing about child-rearing. But after my first column I was inundated with journal articles and story ideas from psychiatrists, psychologists, psychiatric social workers and others in the mental health field. One of my columns was called "The Roots of Shyness." Other subjects ranged from cheating to bedwetting to how Jewish children handle Christmas (mostly with envy), and the knowledge I acquired came in handy when I had my children. A few years later, when Jane Brody came to *The Times* from *The Minneapolis Tribune* and I was a general assignment reporter in the newsroom, she came to my desk. "Are you Martin Tolchin?" she asked. "Guilty as charged," I said. "I expected you to be an old man, with a beard," she said, "I was raised by your columns." And she looked absolutely normal, thank God.

After six years on the Women's Page, located on the ninth floor, I was asked to come down to the third-floor newsroom, the nerve center of the building, as a general-assignment reporter. I wasn't thrilled by the prospect. I'd enjoyed the Women's Page, was developing some expertise and never faced a deadline. It was a much more relaxed pace than the newsroom. If I needed more reporting, I'd just do more interviews, or additional reading. During a lunch at Sardi's, *The Times'* unofficial dining room, Abe Rosenthal and Arthur Gelb offered me what Arthur called "a ringside seat on history." Abe had just returned from overseas to become Metro editor, and Arthur had given up his lifelong ambition to be *The Times'* leading drama critic to become Abe's deputy. The two were likened to Mutt and Jeff. Abe was short and intense; Arthur was tall and lanky, a nervous wreck whom some described as having clenched hair.

PHOTO 3.1 Abe Rosenthal, *The Times'* executive editor, unquestionably the greatest newspaper editor of his time. This brilliant, intense man showed me many kindnesses. (Copyright 1967 *The New York Times*)

When Arthur gave a reporter a story assignment, he often prefaced his remarks by saying, "There's a lot of interest in this story," implying that the publisher had personally requested it, or "Abe wants it done this way." Abe had been a brilliant correspondent, winning a Pulitzer Prize, and Arthur and his wife, Barbara, had written a groundbreaking biography of Eugene O'Neill. When they took over the Metro staff, they couldn't believe how low the salaries were and gave almost everyone a substantial raise. At our lunch, they told me they'd been impressed by my Family articles, and that I belonged on the Metro staff. It also was the gateway to a job as foreign correspondent. Lured by their promises, I reluctantly agreed.

PHOTO 3.2 Arthur Gelb, *The Times'* managing editor, a tall, tower of nerves, whom some said had clenched hair. He was my major mentor at *The Times* and helped me start *The Hill*. (Copyright 2014 *The New York Times*)

The newsroom was a very different place than it is today. It was an enormous room, from 43rd to 44th street, and almost from Broadway to 8th Avenue. Editors summoned reporters using a public address system that was heard throughout the room. The air was filled with smoke, and there were pints of liquor in the drawers of many desks. The Metro staff also had some great editors, including Sheldon Binn, who was lured from the *Daily News*, and Bill Luce, a friend of Jack Kerouac who had hitchhiked across America.

There were several card games in the afternoon. The room was filled with eccentrics. Meyer Berger, a legendary Pulitzer-Prize winner, stood on his desk most afternoons, put his fingers in his mouth and whistled as he danced. Irving Spiegel, who covered religion, performed his newsroom symphony as he walked through the enormous room, starting with calm, guttural sounds and ending in a frenzy.

Sid Zion, the criminal justice reporter, threw a coming out party for a thug convicted of extortion, just released from Sing Sing. It was attended by everybody from the publisher on down. Shortly after the party the thug returned to his bad habits, was convicted and sent back to prison. Sidney later became famous after his daughter's death from what he considered poor treatment by a hospital resident who had worked long hours. He successfully campaigned to limit the hours worked by hospital interns and residents.

When I was a copy boy at *The Times*, there were only two women in the newsroom. It was 1954, and *The Times* had demoted women hired to replace reporters who had gone off to war. Today there are dozens of women, including some top executives including Elisabeth Bumiller, Washington bureau chief; Rebecca Blumenstein who is deputy managing editor; and three women who are assistant managing editors. Similarly, blacks were vastly under-represented, but today Dean Baquet, an extremely talented black journalist, is the paper's executive editor. Like women, black journalists serve in virtually all capacities—foreign and regional correspondents, editors and critics. All media organizations compete for both women and blacks.

Today the eccentrics are mostly gone, liquor bottles are rare, and smoking is prohibited in most newsrooms, which look more like insurance or bank offices. Card games are a thing of the past. Reporters and editors are strapped for time to do their work.

There also were *Times* romances. A top *Times* executive impregnated a reporter, who would bring her son into the newsroom where everyone remarked on how much he resembled his father. The reporter and executive finally reached a financial settlement. There also was a romance between a woman reporter and an assistant managing editor. We all noticed that frequently, when she picked up her phone and dialed, he would pick up his phone, and vice versa. They would both end their calls and hang up their phones at the same time.

It was said that drink was the curse of the (Herald) *Tribune*, and sex was the curse of *The Times*. The seamy Dixie Hotel was across 43rd Street from *The Times*, and on any afternoon some editors frolicked with reporters in the hotel's rundown rooms.

Hazing newcomers was a newsroom tradition, and I wasn't spared. My hours were 1 to 9 p.m., and when I arrived that first day, all the editors were out to lunch. They returned about 2, and I received my first assignments about 2:30. I was assigned three stories: an article about a dispute involving a private cemetery in Queens, including the relevant laws and regulations; an article about a proposed bridge over the East River, including the many types of bridges over the city's rivers; and a few paragraphs on the background of an invasion by an African country into another African country. A summary of each article was expected by 4:30. I was paralyzed. From my desk all I could see were clocks, and by 4:30 I had written not a word. The editors reassigned the bridge and invasion stories, and I barely made the 7 p.m. story deadline with a short article about the cemetery dispute.

In the following weeks I continued to have deadline trouble, and after a couple of months the editors did what they often did to people who can't meet deadlines: they gave me a deadline virtually every minute. I was placed on Night Rewrite, my hours were 7 p.m. to 3 a.m., and my days off were Tuesday and Wednesday. There were murders, riots and other newsworthy events to cover. *The Times* flooded the scenes with reporters who called the Night Rewrite bank of reporters with details. I had no time to think or worry. In those days there was a new edition almost every hour, starting about 10:30, and it was my job to cobble these reports into a story for the next edition, usually a half hour away.

Because of my hours, not only did I not have a ringside seat on history, I never saw my family or friends, and was never sure what meal I should be eating, breakfast, lunch or dinner. I could only date others who worked similar hours, including those who worked in night clubs or Broadway actresses and chorus girls, and sometimes attended cast parties that began at midnight and continued until dawn. At the first anniversary party for "Pajama Game" each guest was given a pair of pajamas decorated with hearts, and a locker in which to place our street clothes. But after 18 months on this job, I could write 1,000 words an hour.

While on Night Rewrite I happened to pass Pennsylvania Station and saw wrecking crews moving into place. I learned that demolition was to begin in a day or two, and successfully lobbied to do the story. My lead said something about a wrecking ball swinging into one of the columns, "crushing the hopes" of those who had vainly sought to save the landmark that made a celebration out of train travel. It was my first page one article.

The 1963–64 World's Fair was my first job after "Night Rewrite." *The Times* had a five-man bureau. I spent my days searching for investigative stories and reported on employees who hadn't been paid, trash that hadn't been picked up and other problems that beset the fair. After several months, Robert Moses, who was the fair's top official, called me in. "More than a million people visited the fair last weekend," he told me. "Didn't *anyone* have a good time?"

While covering the World's Fair I met a beautiful, sweet, smart assistant professor of political science at Brooklyn College. Her name was Susan Goldsmith, and we met at a party in the apartment of Roger Sher, my best friend who was beginning his career as a Wall Street lawyer. She was studying for her PhD at NYU and lived with two other young women in a Greenwich Village apartment. Sue had been dating a brain surgeon, but once we began dating she dropped the physician. Do you know what it means to a Jewish mother to lose a brain surgeon as a potential son-in-law and gain a newspaper reporter? Someone who was divorced and 13 years older? Someone who probably wore a press card in his hatband? Where had they failed? They had given her everything—a Bryn Mawr education, an advanced degree at the University of Chicago, and now this. We were married 50 years, had two children and wrote eight books together. She died in my arms.

Sue's doctoral dissertation was on politics in the New York City police department. One of her classmates was David Durk, an Amherst graduate who was a police detective. He had an unrealistic perception of the police as knights in armor, dedicated to protecting the poor and righting wrongs, and was disillusioned by the corruption that he found in the department. He invited Sue to join him in Harlem at 2 a.m. to see the payoffs to the police, but I persuaded her that such an excursion was far too dangerous.

Durk's partner also was a disillusioned detective. His name was Frank Serpico.

The two detectives tried to involve City Hall in a campaign against corruption. They went to Jay Kriegel, a very young mayoral aide whom they had known casually, who couldn't care less. They finally decided to go to the media, and Sue introduced them to *The New York*

Times. Sylvan Fox was then covering the police department but soon left the paper. The two iconoclasts were inherited by David Burnham, a superb reporter as obsessive as the two detectives. David had been a paratrooper during the Korean War, broken his leg in a jump and then returned to jumping out of military aircraft. Matching their zeal was Arthur Gelb, who by then had succeeded Abe Rosenthal as Metro editor, and he shepherded David's articles into the paper. After *The New York Times* published his first article the mayor appointed a commission to investigate their charges. David's articles were on page one for weeks and resulted in some reforms. Durk was rewarded by being put in a library in Queens, and Serpico was rewarded by being set up by his police colleagues and being shot, almost fatally. Al Pacino played Serpico in the movie.

Robert Moses, who ran the 1963 World's Fair, was the subject of Robert Caro's great book, *The Power Broker.* Although never elected to any position, Moses built many of the parks, beaches and highways throughout the state, cementing his power by giving state legislators and city councilmen the authority to name the architects, engineers and workmen on those projects. He also performed many favors for newspaper publishers. His power even extended to the publisher's office, on the 14th floor of *The Times*, where my coverage of the fair focused on vendors being stiffed and left with unpaid bills, trash that wasn't picked up and other problems.

Eventually Robert Moses exercised his considerable clout and got me reassigned—to Brooklyn, the borough where I was born and spent the first 14 years of my life. But I had no idea it was so large, or so diverse. With three million residents, Brooklyn had a larger population than most of the foreign countries *The Times* covered, yet there was no coverage of the borough where I spent my formative years. I opened a bureau in downtown Brooklyn, and *The Times* gave me a car to travel the length and breadth of the borough. I thought I knew Brooklyn. Wrong. "Only the dead know Brooklyn," wrote Thomas Wolfe. Brooklyn is comprised of dozens of communities, each with its own ethnicity and culture. I did what I had done when I was a copy boy looking for stories: drove to distant communities, walked into laundries, churches, police stations and restaurants and asked, "What's everybody so upset about in this neighborhood?" There always was something. I turned in a steady stream of stories.

One day I went to Coney Island and visited the aquarium. One of the exhibits was a shark tank, and I marveled at the creatures' sharp teeth as they approached the large glass window. The aquarium's director, whom I had asked to meet, showed up as I watched this display. "The New York Bight has the largest number of man-eating sharks in the world," he said. Was that a story, or what? The Bight is the coastline of the Atlantic Ocean from Montauk Point at the tip of Long Island, to halfway down the New Jersey shore. It was home to thousands of residential areas, swim clubs, boardwalks, restaurants and shops. Why was this area teeming with sharks? Because fisherman dropped chum, or fish food, in the water to attract fish, and it ended up attracting sharks. It became one of their breeding grounds. I submitted my story, and the editors were baffled. Where to put it? "This should lead the paper," said one editor, meaning the right hand story on page one. But others felt it would have a devastating effect on thousands of communities and businesses. Finally, they decided to put it on the first page of the Metro section. It caused a stir. A few years later, Peter Benchley wrote *Jaws*. I have no idea whether he had read my story.

After Brooklyn I was back on general assignment. It was August, and I discovered that most psychiatrists took well-deserved vacations that month, leaving their patients to fend for themselves. This led to some desperation on the part of several friends who were in psychoanalysis. My article received a great deal of attention, and I was asked to do a follow-up on where psychiatrists vacationed, and how they spent their vacations. I discovered that one of their main retreats was the Wellfleet-Truro area near the tip of Cape Cod. I was assigned a photographer, Inge Morath, whose husband Arthur Miller would join Sue and me. It was Sue and my first trip together, although we were still not married. I was excited at the prospect of spending a week with Arthur Miller, but that was not to be. His wife became ill and cancelled. Instead I was assigned a *Life* magazine photographer, David Scherman, who lived on the Cape. It was a very good decision. David knew the Cape, especially Wellfleet and Truro, and got us invited to tennis parties, barbecues and all sorts of events attended by shrinks. One tennis party was hosted by Lee Falk, a cartoonist who had created Mandrake the Magician and The Phantom, and also had written and produced Broadway plays. He called his vacation home Xanadu, and it was protected by a huge papier-mâché dragon. We became very good friends. Lee was a man who loved women, and they fully reciprocated. We never had to wait long for a waitress when we were at a restaurant with Lee. The women swarmed over our table. Lee's tennis brunch was attended by lots of psychiatrists as well as his wife, mistress, ex-wife, mother and daughter. He loved them all. As for the psychiatrists, they behaved like all other vacationers, sometimes yelling at their wives and kids, sometimes cheating at tennis with foot faults and bad calls, sometimes opting for a bit of solitude. One sidelight: they loved playing poker with the artists, and invariably lost. It was not the story sought by my editors, who thought they'd be bad parents and difficult spouses, but it ran anyway. I don't know whether Judith Rossner, who wrote the novel *August*, about the disappearance of Manhattan psychiatrists that month, read my article.

Still on general assignment, I received a very interesting assignment that led to my first dispute with Rosenthal. Harrison Salisbury, then an assistant managing editor, had seen that every weekend *The New York Post* carried advertisements for public dances. I was assigned a photographer and told to see what they were all about. The dances were held in the ballrooms of some of New York's best hotels: the Astor, Biltmore and Commodore, among others. I spent an entire weekend dancing my feet off. The women, mostly working class and lower middle class, were a bit embarrassed at being at a public dance to meet men, and they all denied ever having been to one before. I was typing up my notes on a Monday afternoon when Abe came over to me and said that their dress page, the first page of the second section, had gone bust. Could I get my story in that night? I said I'd do my best. Copy boys took my pages as they came out of the typewriter. After about four pages, I was summoned to the Metro desk. "This is a very downbeat story," Abe said. "I was expecting something upbeat, like a cotillion for the poor. If it's so downbeat, why do people go to them?" I said for the same reason that people shopped at Klein's, a discount retailer at Union Square. "They may not like the atmosphere, but they like what they can find there." Abe responded, "I shop at Klein's." Then he told me to finish the story because he had nothing else to put on the dress page. The story ran the following day and took up most of the first page of the second section. I was off Tuesday and Wednesday, fearing the worst. When

I came in Thursday, there was a short note in my mailbox, "See me immediately. Abe." I went up to the desk and Abe said, "I just wanted to tell you, you were right and I was wrong. Whenever you feel that way, I want you to do exactly what you did Monday night: argue with me, tell me why I'm wrong." I often did. I discovered that Abe held emphatic views on many subjects, but, like the excellent reporter he had been, he was educable.

About that time several of us were comparing salaries, and I discovered that I was paid the lowest of all general-assignment reporters. I was still on scale, receiving the minimum required by the Times-Guild contract. Marty Arnold, a very good reporter who later became an editor, said, "That's an outrage. You go up to Abe and say you deserve a raise." Since Marty felt so strongly about it, I felt, who was I to say 'no'? Abe agreed with Marty Arnold, gave me a generous raise on the spot and said, "This is the last time you're ever going to ask me for a raise." And it was. He gave me a raise most years I worked for him.

About six months later I was given a beat: health and hospitals. With the advent of Medicare and Medicaid, in 1965, Abe wanted me to do a takeout, or lengthy article, on the 21 hospitals owned and managed by the city of New York. I asked Dr. Alonzo Yerby, the hospital commissioner and brother of Frank Yerby, the novelist, for a letter requesting that I be treated courteously in the hospitals, allowed to go where I wanted and have all my questions answered. Dr. Yerby refused. When I told Abe, he asked me to deliver the following message to Dr. Yerby: either give me the letter, or he would put a dozen reporters on the beat. Dr. Yerby reluctantly complied. The letter did me little good, however. When I walked in the front door at 9 in the morning, the hospital officials were courteous but barred my entry to certain floors and gave me little information.

I changed tactics. Instead of walking in the front door at 9 in the morning, I walked in the back door at midnight, and talked to the nurses, interns and residents. I visited all 21 hospitals and got an earful. Then I persuaded Dr. Tino Mazzia, chief of anesthesiology at Bellevue, to arrange a meeting with a dozen chiefs of anesthesiology. I told them that the patients knew the hospitals' dilapidated physical conditions, as did the doctors. The only people who didn't know were the citizens of New York City, who ultimately set the budget priorities. If they wanted a bigger share of the city budget, I told them, they had to make the public aware of those conditions. The anesthesiologists were extremely candid. Dr. Mazzia then arranged a meeting with a dozen chiefs of surgery, including my old classmate Mel Worth, who was the chief of surgery at Bellevue. They also were very candid, telling me about the open windows in the operating room at Kings County Hospital with pigeon droppings on the window sills, the supply of IVs that expired and led to deaths, and the shortage of oxygen masks, leading nurses to rotate masks among several patients, which I had observed during my late night forays. The bottom line of my articles was that the city hospitals had excellent medical care that often was undone by a nursing shortage, lack of equipment and the deterioration of the physical plants. The lead of my first article was, "An operating room table collapsed, during surgery, at Morrisania hospital."

Since New York City already was supporting these hospitals, Mayor John Lindsay had determined to put the $35 million in federal Medicaid funds into the general fund, for police, schools and everything else the city paid for. But the public outcry from these articles was so great, the mayor was forced to put the money into the hospitals. It was an example of how the media could change public policy and re-direct the expenditure of public funds. As long as the public was ignorant of conditions in the city hospitals, the bureaucrats could ignore the hospitals' desperate needs. But once the public learned of the true conditions in those hospitals, they forced the power brokers to remedy those conditions.

The articles led to a number of prizes that Sue and I decided to spend on a vacation in England, France, Spain and Portugal. I received one of those prizes, a $5,000 check from the 100-Year Association, made up of companies that had been in New York City for 100 years. The award was given at a black-tie dinner in the grand ballroom of the Waldorf Astoria hotel. I was asked to make a five-minute response, and I told of a previous dinner at the Waldorf Astoria. As high school students, my friend Roger and I had belonged to the Foreign Policy Association, which had monthly Saturday lunches at the hotel featuring a diplomat or other foreign policy expert. We sat in the balcony, content just to listen. During his 1944 election campaign, FDR addressed a black-tie dinner speech before the Foreign

Policy Association at the Waldorf Astoria. Roger and I felt that, as student members of the FPA, we were entitled to hear the speech. We arrived at the ballroom elevators in our customary garb, mackinaws and corduroy slacks, and were immediately surrounded by Secret Service men. "They didn't say a word to us, they didn't put a hand on us, but in a few seconds we were out on the street," I told the audience. "Little did I know that this was good basic training for journalism, where one is not always an invited guest." The anecdote produced appreciative laughter.

I did several follow-up articles, including one about the city hospitals' affiliation with the voluntary hospitals—including Mt. Sinai, Presbyterian and St. Vincent's. I discovered the city was paying for the part-time services of some physicians who never set foot in the city hospitals and also had paid for equipment, including machines used for CT scans and MRIs, which found their way into the voluntary hospitals instead of the city hospitals.

I also did a separate series on the psychiatric wards of the municipal hospitals, which had many of the same problems as the rest of those hospitals. They also had crumbling physical surroundings and a shortage of both personnel and equipment. The patients rarely saw psychiatrists, psychologists or other mental health care personnel. After my articles the city sought to fix the problem, but not to my satisfaction.

I became friendly with state Senator Seymour Thaler of Queens, ranking Democrat on the state Senate health committee, who conducted his own investigation, following my articles. Sy had been a driver for Carmine DeSapio, the Democratic boss alleged to have mob connections, and performed various duties for him during his rise in politics. Sy had a short fuse and bullied his way into hospital facilities. I accompanied him on these visits, along with a few other reporters. At one hospital the reporters were barred entry. No problem, said Thaler, who taped a microphone onto his chest so that we could hear every word while sitting in a nearby van. The hospital ultimately relented. When we came to the operating rooms, hospital officials wanted all of us to remove our clothing and put on blue operating room gowns. Sy refused, unwilling to have hospital officials see the microphone taped to his chest. "Go ahead, Sy," we teased. "Take off your suit and put on a gown." The reporters finally formed a circle around Sy, so that he could undress without the microphone being seen by the hospital officials. Sy later was a prime source for Sue's and my first book, on political patronage. Sy ultimately was elected to the state Supreme Court, but never served. Although married to a very rich woman, Sy wanted to pay off the political leaders with his own money. To do this, he used Treasury bills. Unfortunately, they had been stolen. It was a crime almost guaranteed to be detected. Sy ended up in the federal prison in Danbury, Conn., where he died of a heart attack.

The hospitals of course struck back. *The Times* publisher was on several hospital boards and his friends, relatives and other elites were on most of the others. They came to *The Times* to protest, arguing I was undermining confidence in the city's hospitals. I later learned of a meeting they had with Turner Catledge, then *The Times'* managing editor, a smooth-talking southerner and an excellent politician. I went to Catledge to protest the protests, saying that I should have been at those meetings. "Marty," he said, "We had confidence in your reporting, so there was no need." Was he a politician or what?

I was invited, however, to a publisher's lunch with the hospitals commissioner and his deputy. The lunch was in the publisher's board room, attended by the publisher and all the top editors. Dr. Yerby, the commissioner, began by saying that thanks to my stories, his department was being investigated by the state Senate, the state Assembly, the city's investigations commissioner and a blue-ribbon commission appointed by the governor. He added that my investigation was the toughest.

Notwithstanding what I took for praise, immediately after the meeting I suffered an almost disabling anxiety attack. I thought I was having a heart attack, except that I didn't feel anything in my jaw or arms. These attacks continued during the next several days. I went to see a psychiatrist. I didn't know any, so I went to the president of the American Psychiatric Association, a psychiatrist who had testified in several major court trials. He put me on Librium, an anti-anxiety drug, and the attacks promptly ended. Also, I felt a little dopey, as if I was seeing life through a gauze bandage. I felt like I was just going through the motions. After a month, I decided to go off the drug. My attacks immediately returned, but I decided to tough it out, and in a couple of days they were gone. So was the gauzy effect. I no longer felt dopey.

Still reporting on the health field, I received a tip from a source at the Health Department that a Park Avenue dentist who gave patients a general anesthetic just had his second anesthetic death. He was good at putting patients under, but not at bringing them out of their sleep. I wrote a summary and was called to the desk. "Why don't we wait until he has a third death?" Arthur said, as Abe nodded his head in agreement. I was upset. I thought it was a good story and would be a public service to run it. Then Abe said, "Arthur and I go to a Park Avenue dentist. What's his name?" I said, "If you don't think the readers of *The New York Times* are entitled to know, I don't think you're entitled to know," and stormed back to my desk and ran down the back stairway to the street. I then heard footsteps running after me, and Arthur's voice, "Marty, Marty, you win. We'll run the story."

About that time a friend of mine gave birth to a daughter. I went to visit her at Mt. Sinai hospital's maternity ward, and found the ward overflowing with patients. My friend and a number of other women didn't even have a hospital room or bed; instead they were placed on gurneys in the corridor. I asked a maternity nurse if it were always like that, and she said she had never before seen such an overflow. She noted that it was nine months after New York City's blackout, and the northeast's worst electrical outage. I checked with the city hospital department and a number of private hospitals. Their maternity wards all were overflowing, with the largest number of maternity patients in their history. I then wrote a story about these Blackout Babies, which ran on page one with a quote from a sociologist, "The lights went out, and people interacted with each other in the dark." About a month later, I received a letter from a major Hollywood studio. Would I come out to Hollywood and write a screenplay about the Blackout Babies? Sue and I thought long and hard, but ultimately I decided to stay at *The Times*. A few years later, a movie was made, called "The Night the Lights Went Out." How different my life would have been had I taken the offer.

Perhaps because of my hospital stories, Abe and Artie decided to make me City Hall bureau chief. The current bureau chief, Paul Crowell, was retiring.

He'd held the job for more than 20 years and knew just about everything there was to know about the city's politics and economics. He was such a fixture that mayors' chauffeurs drove him home at night. *The Times* bureau had six reporters, some of whom also had been there quite a while and expected to get promoted to bureau chief. Two decided to retire, and the rest were none too pleased to have a 30-something as their boss. My appointment also stunned many of the reporters for other media outlets at City Hall. The reporters worked in "Room 9," a grungy, littered room reminiscent of the newsroom in "The Front Page." Pinup photos adorned the walls, and liquor bottles were common in the desks. Chaos reigned, with lobbyists walking in and out and reporters yelling into their phones. I attended numerous farewell parties in honor of my predecessor, and the toasts invariably included the question, "Why is *The Times* replacing a giant with a pygmy?" meaning me. In the early days, the other, older reporters sent the Metro desk a schedule of expected stories before I got in. The schedule was my job, and I quickly put an end to that practice.

John Vliet Lindsay, a product of St. Paul's and Yale, was mayor when I arrived at City Hall. He was a handsome, athletic, liberal Republican who had represented Manhattan's Upper East Side, the so-called Silk Stocking District, in Congress. In contrast to most reporters, who were paunchy and balding, Lindsay had a full head of hair and a magnificent body, which he displayed diving into community swimming pools. He walked the city's streets with his shirtsleeves rolled up and his jacket thrown over a shoulder. What a difference from the Tammany pols who had long controlled City Hall. His campaign poster had a photograph of him walking the city streets, with a quote from Murray Kempton, the great columnist, "He is fresh, and everyone else is tired."

I began with great admiration for the mayor, but in time my ardor diminished. I've always had a weakness for politicians, whether liberal or conservative. They're in the arena, trying to influence the great decisions of the day. Most enjoy people and are invigorated by them. And most genuinely want to serve the public, especially in their early years, when service is more important to them than winning elections. In time this balance changes, as they realize that it's difficult to get anything done without compromising, and compromise becomes a way of life. Some forget why they entered the arena in the first place. Indeed, John Lindsay taught me never to give my heart to a politician; he'll break it every time. If you must, give your heart to an artist or musician or someone in the healing professions, or even a journalist. But never a politician.

Lindsay was a good showman, with a flair for publicity. Walking the city's streets and diving into community swimming pools resulted in page one photographs in the city's nine newspapers. So did his liberal remarks. He showed off his acting ability every February at the annual dinner of the Inner Circle, comprised of the city's political reporters. After the reporters presented various skits, the mayor would put on a top hat or straw hat, take the stage with the cast of a current Broadway hit and sing made-up lyrics to the musical hits of the day.

The Inner Circle shows were a temporary truce in the mayor's constant battle with the City Hall press corps. To some extent it was a class difference. Very few City Hall reporters had gone to prep school. Not too many had attended Ivy League colleges; indeed, many had never gone to college. Many were old school, working class guys (no women), and had served many years in their jobs. Some reporters doubled as press agents for the city councilmen they covered. Their workspace, Room 9, was a pig sty. The mayor clearly had disdain for those who, to some extent, held his future in their hands. Life is unfair.

In a temper tantrum, Lindsay closed the restroom used by the reporters, who then had to either climb a flight to another restroom or go to another building a few minutes away. In short order, however, Lindsay reversed himself and cut a ceremonial tape to reopen the restroom. "In the future," he said, "all the leaks will be here." One episode the City Hall reporters long remembered: one frigid evening, during a strike, the mayor was meeting with union officials at Gracie Mansion, the mayor's official residence, overlooking the East River. It was snowing, but the reporters were not allowed inside the mansion, instead forced to wait outside as the temperature plummeted and the snow intensified. Some of the reporters were older, while others had health problems. No matter. Our requests to be allowed inside, in an unused room, were denied. The mayor finally relented, after more than an hour, and we were admitted to a lobby, without chairs, sofas or any kind of seating. To the City Hall reporters, the

PHOTO 3.3 Mayor John Lindsay. The mayor looks none too happy giving me an award: the Schaefer Gold (plated) Typewriter. Lindsay gave me a valuable lesson in politics: never give your heart to a politician. Rudy Schaefer, president of the brewery, is on the left.

(Susan Tolchin photo)

episode epitomized the contempt with which the mayor regarded them, which was fully reciprocated. It did nothing to improve the mayor's public relations.

In a peace offering, the mayor granted me an interview. He kept me waiting in an anteroom, along with another man who also had an appointment. We got to talking, and I asked what he was seeing the mayor about. He said that he wanted to renew his consulting contract. Who knew that the mayor farmed out consulting contracts? The city's personnel included experts on just about every subject. Many had begun working for the city during the Depression and had PhDs. It turned out that the mayor gave those contracts to firms that had done work for him, including polling and focus groups, during his re-election campaign.

After the interview I went to the controller's office and found the contracts. One of them, done by a prestigious consulting firm, was a study of transportation in and out of the city. Its major finding: traffic came into the city in the morning, and went out of the city in late afternoon and evening. For this the city paid hundreds of thousands of dollars. I wrote several articles about these contracts, which the mayor protested. He finally asked to see the executive editor, now Abe Rosenthal, and arrived in Abe's boardroom with a coterie of city officials. I had no idea what he would criticize, and brought my notes, in folders in about five cardboard cartons, necessitating five trips. Everybody watched as I brought them in one at a time. Then Abe told Lindsay he had the floor. In words I will always remember, Lindsay said, "We have no quarrel with any of the facts in Marty's stories, but their entire thrust is anti-intellectual, know-nothing-ism, and Beamism," referring to Abe Beame, the city's controller. The implication was that I wore a green eye-shade and lacked the knowledge and intelligence to appreciate the consulting contracts. After the mayor's statement, I heaved a huge sigh of relief. Abe Rosenthal responded: "Mr. Mayor, if you have no problem with any of the facts in Marty's story, I don't think we have much to talk about." And that was that.

I also discovered why few politicians die poor. I had decided to compare the city and state's investment portfolios and saw that while they were similar, there were some marked differences. There were, of course, investments in companies controlled by big donors, which I had expected. I also discovered that the state had a substantial investment in Macy's department stores, R.H. Macy & Co., while the city had none. I asked Mario Procaccino, the city's controller, to explain the difference. He told me that, as a matter of fact, the city intended to purchase R. H Macy stock the following week. By the time I returned to my office, Procaccino already had left three messages. "You know, Marty, what I told you was in strict confidence." It then dawned on me how someone could be enriched by knowledge of such a future purchase. When the city or state purchased stock, it was for tens of thousands of shares, and moved the markets. With advance knowledge of such a sale, politicians could purchase stock, whose price was bound to increase. Indeed, I checked the stock after the purchase and sure enough, the price had soared. This was in the

1970s, before federal and state prosecutors sharpened their attacks on insider trading. In the old days, city fathers had inside information on where the city would build subway or trolley lines, and purchased land along those routes.

Despite my growing antipathy to Lindsay, I became friendly with Tom Morgan, his press secretary. Tom had been an excellent reporter and writer for the old *Look* magazine and had written a very good novel. But he worked for Lindsay. He called me at home about 10 o'clock one night and said he had obtained a copy of Governor Rockefeller's budget which had sharp cuts in funding for the city. He cited chapter and verse. The mayor and governor had been on a collision course almost since Lindsay's election. Their personalities were too alike. I called the Metro desk and got the story into the paper's late editions. It landed on page one. When I got into work the next morning, all hell had broken loose. Rockefeller adamantly denied the story and released the city portion of his budget to prove his point. Clearly, I had been had. I called Tom and he promised to call me back. Abe Rosenthal said that, although I had promised Tom confidentiality, I had to out him as my source because he had given me bad information. I was reluctant to do that, but Abe insisted. After that incident, I initiated a policy: I would take nothing off-the-record. I told Lindsay officials that I could be standing next to the mayor in a City Hall urinal, and if he told me something important, I would report it. And I did. Postscript: Tom later married Mary Rockefeller, one of the governor's children. The governor made a cameo appearance at the wedding and reception.

Many of Lindsay's problems involved Jews. In a searing dispute, the mayor proposed a massive housing project in Forest Hills, Queens: three skyscrapers that would bring thousands of welfare recipients into the middle of a quiet, Jewish middle-class neighborhood. The residents vigorously objected, fearing that the newcomers would bring crime and otherwise forever change their neighborhood. They asked: if Lindsay was so intent on building these skyscrapers, why not build them across the street from Gracie Mansion? They were denounced as racists. In fact, I had a strong argument with some of my editors, who felt the same way. It happened at a dinner party in Montclair, N.J., where we lived, and lasted until 3 in the morning. I pointed out that the editors transcended their neighborhoods, mostly in Manhattan and close-in suburbs. They sent their children to private schools, seldom took public transportation and didn't rely on local restaurants or theaters. But neighborhoods meant a great deal to Forest Hills residents. Their children went to public schools, they took the subway to work—not cars, taxis or limousines—patronized local bars and restaurants, and went to local movie houses.

The mayor, responding to criticism, appointed a virtually unknown Queens lawyer, Mario Cuomo, to mediate the dispute. I ran into Mario in the City Hall lobby, where he was waiting to give Lindsay his recommendations. I asked what he had recommended. He asked what I would do. I said I'd cut the housing in half and make the apartment houses half as high. "That's what I'm recommending," he said. I immediately contacted the Metro desk, and prepared to write the story. After the editorial board phoned Mario for further explanation, he called me. "I haven't even given the mayor my recommendation yet," he said. I told him that it was too late to stop *The Times* story and editorial. We had beaten everyone else to the story. Of course, Mario went on to become a very good governor of New York. Some Forest Hills residents fled to the suburbs, and the reduced housing project opened without incident in 1975.

Another dispute involved a school board in the Ocean Hill-Brownsville section of Brooklyn. In a desire to give blacks and other minorities more power, the mayor gave them control of a community school board. The newly constituted school board fired Jewish principals and teachers. It was an experiment in self-government. The teachers' union promptly went on a city-wide strike, a battle that lasted from May to November 1968, when the state took control of the board and reinstated the Jewish principals and teachers.

I also reported on the City Council. In one dramatic debate, Ted Weiss, then a very young councilman. made an impassioned, liberal speech, when up from the back benches arose Dominic L. Corso, a wholly owned subsidiary of the Bronx Democratic Party. "You young fellows think it takes guts to stand up for what you think is right?" Corso bellowed. "Let me tell you something. That doesn't take guts. What really takes guts is to stand up for what you know is wrong."

The City Hall bureau worked especially hard, including weekends, around budget time. One year, after the budget stories had run their course, and with the City Council off on its annual golf picnic, we were told that the news lid was on until 4 p.m., meaning that no news would be coming out of City Hall at least until then. Appreciative of the hard work the bureau had put in and of the time we now had to ourselves, I took the entire City Hall bureau to an afternoon game at Shea Stadium to see the Mets play the Cincinnati Reds. All six of us walked into the newsroom a little after 4. Gil Hagerty, a Metro desk News clerk, greeted me by saying, "Boy, are you in trouble." It turned out that one of the councilmen, George Swetnick, a friend of mine, had a heart attack and died on the golf course. Arthur Gelb, then Metro editor, had called City Hall numerous times, but this was before cell phones and voice mail. He couldn't reach anyone. Arthur called me into his small office. Where had we been? Sensing that my career at *The Times* was at an end, I told him. "Let me get this straight," Arthur said. "You're telling me that you, the City Hall bureau chief, on company time and company pay, took the entire City Hall bureau to a baseball game?" he asked. "That's about the size of it," I replied. He hesitated, banged his fist on his desk and said, "That's wonderful, Marty. What a morale booster. I want you to put this on your expense account." I did, but carefully camouflaged, not as a baseball game.

Arthur had boundless curiosity, so it was not surprising that he wanted to see the first major porno film, "Deep Throat," playing at the World Theater, Broadway and 49th Street, just a few blocks from the office. He took half a dozen reporters with him. Back in the newsroom, Fred Ferretti, a wonderful reporter who had not been invited, pulled off a prank. He called the theater and asked them to page Arthur. An usher walked up and down the aisles, shouting, "Telephone call for Arthur Gelb, metropolitan editor of *The New York Times*."

Every Wednesday morning I was invited to a meeting of *The Times'* political reporters. One week I attended the meeting after interviewing Stanley Steingut, Speaker of the New York State Assembly and long-time Brooklyn Democratic leader. The interview was interrupted several times by telephone calls, and I of course could only hear Steingut's end of the conversations: "Yes, Max, you get the electrical contracts, but Harry gets the plumbing, Sam gets the heating and air conditioning, Joe gets the cafeteria." During a pause in the calls, I said, "Mr. Steingut, I couldn't help overhear your end of the conversations. Were you talking about a public building or a private building?" Steingut gave me his 14 karat smile and asked, "Does it really matter?" Few politicians die poor.

Fresh from the interview, I went to one of our political meetings. The topic was, "Why do people go into politics?" Who needed all the scrutiny and vilification that comes with being a politician? The veteran reporters all noted that most politicians were wealthy, and said, in essence, "They just want to give back." I took exception, and said, "They just want to get more," citing my interview with Steingut. Sensing a story, Arthur Gelb, who succeeded Abe as Metro editor, asked me to follow up with a takeout on the subject. I found that many politicians in the city and state were, like Steingut, in it for themselves, and cited chapter and verse. When my article ran, I received six calls from book publishers before noon. The last one was from Jason Epstein of Random House. I was unaware of his history and reputation. Jason was the founder of the quality paperback, one of the founders of the N.Y. Review of Books and a heavyweight in the field of publishing. I told him that I'd already made appointments to see five other publishers, and asked him to wait until this round was over. He said, "Why not see me first?" Fortunately, I did. I didn't see how I could write a book and devote the necessary time and energy to *The Times*, so I asked Sue to partner with me. She readily agreed. In academe it's publish or perish. At lunch, Epstein offered us a modest advance, even for 1968: $5,000, which we used as the down payment for our first house, a five-bedroom center hall colonial on a tree-lined street in Montclair, N.J., that cost $31,250. I was nervous about writing a book, so I sent Jason the first few chapters. He invited Sue and me to lunch. "You're writing this like a newspaper story, as if you have to say everything in 800 words," he said. "This is a book. You have all the space you need. I want you to hold every idea, every anecdote, every observation up to the light, and describe all the facets until you go to the next idea or anecdote. And I don't want to see a paragraph of less than 500 words."

It was great advice, and I've given it to many newspaper buddies writing their first book. Before publication, I sent the galley proofs to several publications including *The Times*' magazine, *New York* magazine and *The New Yorker*. I told them that I would take the first offer.

Clay Felker, the brilliant editor of *New York* magazine, was the first to respond, and at lunch told us that he wanted three excerpts, the first of which was featured on the cover, with the headline: "The Price of a Judgeship in N.Y." The price was about a year's salary given to the political leader. About six weeks after my letter, *The Times* responded. I told them that I already sold the magazine rights to *New York* magazine. *The Times* editors were outraged. The book, *To the Victor: Political Patronage from the Clubhouse to the White House*, has been cited in five decisions by justices of the U.S. Supreme Court. Each time we were cited, I wrote to the justice saying how thrilled we were that he cited us, and asked for some memorabilia, "your judicial gown, your pen, or a signed copy of the opinion." Every justice except Antonin Scalia sent a signed copy of the opinion, but Scalia, whose daughter was a Bryn Mawr classmate of my daughter Karen, who started a humor magazine there, also sent a letter. It reads, in part, "I know how hard it is to be humorous at Bryn Mawr these days."

As with most of our books, we changed our mind 180 degrees about patronage. When we began, we thought it was inherently corrupt, and the merit system was the best way to appoint people, and award government contracts. When we finished, we realized it was the grease that made politics function, and those who felt morally superior and disdained patronage found it difficult to govern.

How do you write a book with your wife? Very carefully. We worked on a jerry-rigged desk in our attic, a door supported by bricks. We divided the chapters, did the interviewing and writing, and then exchanged chapters. Sue and I exchanged our first chapters on that desk with our newborn son Charlie in the middle as a neutral zone. Sue came from academe and edited my chapter with small, marginal notes. But I came from a newsroom and used a red pencil and sometimes threw out entire pages. I looked up and saw that Sue was not happy. Tears were beginning to form. I realized that more than a book was at stake. I saw ourselves giving back the advance, selling the house and giving up the baby. Thenceforth we adopted a new strategy, editing in private and prefacing our remarks by saying, "Sweetheart, this is the most incisive thing ever written about cost benefit analysis. Darling, you can search the literature and not find anything on the subject written with such nuance and insight. But dearest, if I can venture one small suggestion, just to bring to the fore the ideas that you have so brilliantly developed . . . it really starts on page 25."

In August, 1968, our son Charlie came along. He was a robust 6 pounds 8 ounces, but had a problem. He wasn't evacuating properly. This was a symptom of Cystic Fibrosis, a fatal disease we had never heard of, in which thicker–than–normal mucous clogs the body's breathing apparatus. In early childhood, Charlie's stools were extremely loose, a sign he had not digested all his food. He also had a persistent cough. Sue took him to the best pediatricians in New York, who told her she was a neurotic parent. So was I. But when I got transferred to Washington, a doctor friend recommended a full checkup for Charlie. We took him to Johns Hopkins where a resident asked if he'd ever had a Sweat Test. No, we'd never even heard of a Sweat Test. It's for CF. Charlie flunked the test. The average mortality was 8 years old. We were reeling.

I couldn't do any work. I would come into *The Times* office in the morning, check my mail and phone messages, and then spend the day walking around the city, mostly around the Tidal Basin. I would return to *The Times* office in late afternoon and go home. I did this for a month, and nobody said anything.

The National Institutes of Health was just beginning an in–house program for young CF patients. We went to be interviewed by a young post–doc, who told us, "If the cause of CF was discovered tomorrow, and the cure the day after tomorrow, it would be too late to help your child." He then told Sue she had to quit her job, because Charlie would require her full attention, but that would last only a year or so, when she'd have a nervous breakdown. He would be dead in three years, we were told. Meanwhile, I would have fled the scene, because most fathers of chronically ill children flee their marriage and their kids. We left determined never to allow our son to be treated at NIH. Fortunately, we found a wonderful CF doctor, Lucas Kylshiski, at Children's Hospital. He slapped Charlie's x-rays over the fluorescent light panel and declared, "Your son will graduate high school and college, and will have a career."

Dr. Kylshiski was right. Charlie went to Duke and George Washington universities, and loved his job as an advertising copywriter. He had a double lung transplant that extended his life six years, and died two weeks before his 35th birthday. His sister Karen, meanwhile, followed in her mother's footsteps, and worked in academe as an associate professor. Unlike Sue, whose field was government, Karen's field was English, including movies and coming of age novels.

At about this time, Lindsay switched parties. A career Republican, he became a Democrat and began a campaign for the presidency. But the enemies he had made, especially among the city's Jews, caught up with him. At a campaign stop in Miami Beach, someone paid for a plane to fly back and forth along the coast. The plane had a trailer that could easily be read by those attending a Lindsay campaign rally. The sign said, "Lindsay spells Tsouris." Tsouris is Yiddish for trouble.

In August 1972, we began our annual month-long vacation in Wellfleet, on Cape Cod, when Bob Sherrill, a magazine writer and friend, called with a news tip. Senator George McGovern of South Dakota was the Democratic nominee for president and selected Senator Tom Eagleton of Missouri as his running mate. But Eagleton was forced to drop out after the disclosure that he had undergone shock treatment for mental illness. Sherrill's tip: Vice President Spiro Agnew had been seeing a New York physician, Dr. Max Jacobson, aka Dr. Feelgood, for amphetamines. I called Arthur who told me to return immediately to New York. That was the end of my vacation.

Apparently, one of Dr. Feelgood's former nurses had disclosed Agnew's treatment to the nurse's psychiatrist, a friend of Sherrill's. Gene Roberts, *The Times'* national editor, and I took the train to Westport to the psychiatrist's office. He was reluctant to give us the nurse's name or whereabouts. "*The Times* is not an eleemosynary institution, and neither am I," the psychiatrist said. He wanted to be paid. *The Times* had a rule: never pay for information. We saw the psychiatrist every 50 minutes, during his 10 minutes between patients, and kept an open line to New York to discuss our response with the publisher and executive editor. We finally reached an agreement: we wouldn't pay the psychiatrist money, but we would quote him in articles that we wrote about his specialty. We then found and interviewed the nurse, who confirmed Sherrill's information. But we needed a second confirmation. We staked out Dr. Feelgood's office, but to no avail. We did, however, discover that his patients included President Kennedy, Jackie Kennedy and most of the Kennedy clan. He had been photographed on the Kennedy's yacht. Other patients included celebrities including Alan Jay Lerner, who wrote the lyrics for "My Fair Lady," "Paint Your Wagon" and many other Broadway hits.

By the end of 1972, I felt so antagonistic toward Lindsay that I felt I couldn't cover him fairly. I asked to be relieved, perhaps with a foreign assignment. Abe offered me Nairobi, covering sub-Saharan Africa, or Asia. In Africa, he said, I'd be away from home about 75% of the time and in Asia, perhaps 80%. When I got home, I excitedly told Sue, "Pack your bags, honey, we're going to see some of this world." But when I told her about the amount of time I'd be away from home, she became far less enthusiastic. "Do you really want to be an absentee husband and father?" she asked. "Do you really want to miss your son's soccer games and your daughter's ballet performances?" So, I turned down these jobs. Then Abe asked, "How'd you like to go to Washington?" "How much travel?" I asked. Abe said minimal, except during political campaign season. I was hooked.

My last major story on the Metro staff was an investigative article on the south Bronx. A living ruin, the area had been the victim of the South Bronx Expressway. Buildings had been torn down to make way for the new highway, and what remained looked like bombed out Paris or Berlin after World War II. People lived in buildings without water or electricity, gangs ran wild, and Manhattan criminal enterprises paid $5 to South Bronx children to murder those who threatened their empires. I spent three weeks in the south Bronx, and had to urinate so frequently I thought I had a bladder infection. But the constant urination disappeared as soon as I returned to my desk at *The Times*. I delivered a lengthy article to Arthur Gelb, then Metro editor, at his home in Manhattan. By the time I returned to my home in Montclair, N.J., he had called me several times, to congratulate me. He divided my article into five sections, and each ran on page one on successive days. Then I was ready for new challenges, and the move to Washington.

4

WASHINGTON, HERE I COME

In March 1973, I received a telephone call from Representative Ben Rosenthal's press secretary, inviting me to the congressman's son's Bar Mitzvah in Washington. Rosenthal was a Democrat from Queens. "I don't know the congressman," I told him, "and besides, I live in Montclair, N.J." "Not for long," was the response. The press secretary told me I was about to be transferred to the Washington bureau, to be a regional reporter and cover the congressional delegations from New York, N.J. and Connecticut, and what the Administration was planning for our area. That was how I found out about my next assignment. My official notice came a few days later. I later told this story eulogizing Ben in a ceremony in the Capitol Rotunda.

A few days before my move, in April 1973, I learned that almost the entire Washington bureau had signed a petition to Abe protesting my transfer to their bureau. Why? Mario Biaggi, a congressman from Queens, was running for mayor. I discovered that he had been called before a grand jury and taken the Fifth Amendment, and I had reported that fact. *The Times* petitioners considered grand jury proceedings inviolate, and said that I had violated Biaggi's rights, as well as the Constitution. Biaggi was ultimately convicted of a crime and sentenced to two and a half years in prison. When I asked Abe about the petition, he told me not to worry about it. "Remember, this is the bureau that missed Watergate," he said. Indeed, the bureau had left almost the entire investigation to *The Washington Post*, which won a Pulitzer Prize for its role in the investigation that led to the resignation of President Nixon. *The Times* bureau was a victim of old-fashioned journalism. Max Frankel, the bureau chief, and James "Scotty" Reston, *The Times'* celebrated columnist, lunched regularly with Henry Kissinger, who had continually assured them that there was nothing to *The Post's* Watergate stories.

The New York delegation was a journalistic feast. There was Bella Abzug, the great feminist, who, when told by William "Fishbait" Miller, the House Sergeant at Arms, to remove one of her outsized hats before she entered the House chamber, responded, "Fuck You," and strode in, hat and all. The delegation had two outstanding senators, Jacob Javits, a Republican, and later Daniel Patrick Moynihan, a Democrat. Four members of the Brooklyn delegation, all Democrats, were convicted of white collar crimes while I was a regional reporter: Representatives Bert Podell, Frank Brasco, Fred Richmond and John Murphy. Robert Garcia, a Bronx Democrat, also was convicted. Others whom I covered who were convicted of crimes included two New Jersey Democrats: Senator Harrison Williams and Representative Frank Thompson.

Before I moved to Washington, I dropped by to introduce myself to Javits, one of his party's few liberals. His New York City office was in the Grand Central Terminal office building. "Are you married?" Javits asked. When I told him I was, he said, "I had hoped we could have dinner together a few times a week." I told him I liked having dinner with my family but said we could have breakfast together as often as he liked. And we did. Javits was very smart, an intellectual who was well read and enjoyed discussing politics, literature and art. He also loved publicity. With several committee meetings scheduled for the same time, he would travel from one to the other until he found TV cameras and then settle in. Javits also had a great staff, including Patricia Shakow and Steve Kurzman.

I quickly learned the difference between being a reporter in New York and in Washington. In New York, reporters are on the outside looking in. In Washington, they're invited to the dinner table. Ben Rosenthal wasn't the only member of Congress to invite us to dinner. Also issuing an invitation before we arrived was Representative

Ogden Reid Jr., a New York Republican and scion of the family that owned the *New York Herald Tribune*. He planned to run for governor. It turned out to be a small dinner party. Also present were former Supreme Court Justice Abe Fortas and his wife, Carolyn Agger; Secretary of Commerce Harry Dent and his wife; and the Israeli ambassador to the U.S. and his wife. After dinner, there was a discussion of Washington friendships.

"I have hundreds of acquaintances," Carolyn Agger said, as she lit a thin cigar, "but you could count my real friends on the fingers of one hand and have some left over." Why? In Washington, social life was a continuation of political life, glitzy but not especially nutritious. At another dinner party a few weeks later, I was talking to the hostess on the back deck of a lavish home in Cleveland Park, overlooking a magnificent garden. "What a beautiful house," I said, "and you have so many friends." She said, "Friends? They're not my friends. How many would come to my funeral?"

William Safire, my high school buddy, joined *The Times*' Washington bureau when I did, in April 1973, to begin his 30-plus years as a conservative columnist and wordsmith. We were both pariahs. I was resented because of my grand jury articles, and also because my friendship with Abe Rosenthal led my new colleagues to fear that Rosenthal had put me in the bureau as a spy. *The Times*' New York headquarters had long been at odds with the Washington bureau, protected by James Reston, one of the most eminent columnists of his day. Bill Safire was resented because he had been a Nixon speechwriter, and virtually every member of the bureau thought that he or she should be anointed a columnist, not Safire. In the absence of invitations from our new colleagues, Bill and I frequently lunched together.

Shortly after I arrived in the bureau, I sent a letter to the six senators and 60 house members from New York, New Jersey and Connecticut, whom I was sent to cover, requesting both their net worth statements and their recently filed tax returns. The New York congressional delegation held several meetings on how to respond. Those most upset about my request were the least wealthy members, ashamed to let their constituents know how little money they had. Overall, about one-third gave me everything I had requested, one-third gave me one or the other document, and one-third told me to go to hell. Firmly in the latter camp was Senator James Buckley, a Republican and staunch conservative like his brother, William Buckley. Senator Buckley held a news conference to denounce me and *The Times* for "invasion of privacy." I had sent the offending letter on my own, without clearing it with either Clifton Daniel, the Washington bureau chief, or Abe Rosenthal, executive editor. When reporters went to Rosenthal seeking a response to Senator Buckley's charge, Abe said, "This is the first I've heard of Marty's letter, but I don't see how it's an invasion of privacy to *request* information." The information I gleaned from those documents formed the basis of a series of articles.

At the same time, I wrote to every cabinet member asking what they had planned for New York, New Jersey and Connecticut. To my amazement, I obtained several interviews, which also led to a series of articles. I also discovered a government pamphlet, published annually, "Federal Aid to the States," which described the financial aid given the states. I compared New York to California and Illinois, which also had large populations as well as both urban and rural areas, and found that those states received much more federal aid than New York. I asked New York officials why the state was discriminated against, and they blamed President Nixon's anti-New York stance. I then asked government officials the reason, and they said that New York seldom made formal requests for aid, and on the rare occasions when they did so, they seldom met deadlines. This led to a series of articles. My strategy was reminiscent of Ben Hecht's strategy when he was a young newspaper reporter in Chicago. Hecht dug up a series of long forgotten unsolved murders and wrote stories about them without mentioning that they had occurred long ago. He described this tactic in his autobiography, "A Child of the Century," in a chapter titled, "I Start a Crime Wave." Like Hecht's crusade, my articles on the disparity in federal funding could have been written decades earlier.

I enjoyed being *The Times'* regional reporter in Washington, although I was entirely shut out of the major story of those years: Watergate. I nevertheless had a good run of page one stories, and in short order became accepted by the Washington bureau. My articles were edited in both Washington and New York, where the best of the copy editors, Irv Molotsky, became a good friend. Bill Safire also was accepted by the bureau. At a bureau summer party at an editor's home, a reporter's young son fell into a pool and Bill dove in, fully dressed, to rescue the child. Bill later admitted that his beautiful wife, Helene, a British import, had pushed him into the pool. After that, few resented his presence in the bureau, or his column. "It was hard to hate me after that," Bill said. Bill always was generous, sharing tips and insights with bureau reporters. Bill was especially generous to me. He redefined the meaning of friendship.

I went back to New York City for day trips, talking to city and state officials about what the federal government was doing to them. When Charlie and Karen were about 10, I started taking them separately on a business trip a year. The first time, I took Charlie to New York to interview several congressmen from Long Island. It was a snowy, miserable day. When the Eastern Shuttle took off, Charlie said, "Dad, this is going to be the best day of my whole, entire life." We returned in early evening, without having had supper. As we were landing, Charlie looked at the Capitol and Washington Monument,

PHOTO 4.1 Senator Ted Kennedy. He was wonderful with my kids, whom I brought to an interview, at which he was extremely nervous. (Author's photo)

both illuminated, and said, "Dad, this *was* the best day of my whole, entire life." Lunch with Mayor Koch was a favorite, and Karen still remembers the sundaes we had at Rumplemayer's after our City Hall lunch with Mayor Koch. I also took them with me when I interviewed celebrities like Henry Kissinger, Tip O'Neil or Ted Kennedy. I thought it was worth the day of school they missed.

About a year after I arrived in Washington, New York Governor Nelson Rockefeller began inviting me to breakfast in the Senate dining room whenever he came to town. We both dished the dirt. I told him what I knew about Nixon's plans for the state, and the state of Washington politics, and he gave me information on state initiatives that could be impacted by the federal government. His breakfast seldom wavered: orange juice, eggs, toast and coffee with milk and sugar. He would absently remove his glasses and stir his coffee with the stem. I once told him that my mother wouldn't approve of that

PHOTO 4.2 Governor Nelson Rockefeller. We dished the dirt at breakfast in the senator's dining room when, as governor, he came to Washington. This was our first meeting, on his private plane. (Governor's staff photo)

stirring, and he said, "Neither would mine." Those breakfasts produced a raft of stories.

These days I hear some friends and political observers lament the lack of civility in Congress and harken back to the supposedly "good old days." But I quickly learned that politics had always been a blood sport, and the "good old days" never existed. When I arrived in the Capitol, in April 1973, Congress was dominated by southern reactionary bigots, who chaired nearly all the important committees. Their leader was Richard Russell, a Democrat of Georgia, who has a Senate office building named after him. Other southern powerhouses included Senators James Eastland and John Stennis of Mississippi, Strom Thurmond of South Carolina, Jesse Helms of North Carolina, Russell Long of Louisiana, John McClellan of Arkansas, John Sparkman of Alabama, and Sam Ervin of North Carolina. They ran the Senate with iron fists beneath velvet gloves. Unfailingly polite, exceedingly courteous, they nevertheless made it clear that anyone who questioned their authority would find it difficult to find funds for their pet projects, and nearly impossible to get to turn their legislative proposals into law. Indeed, newcomers were chastised for even venturing an opinion. Today, with television and the diffusion of chairmanships to senators and House members from all regions with differing ideologies, and 24/7 coverage of Congress, the institution has become more democratized, and with democratization has come inevitable differences of opinion that are now expressed, not stifled.

My very first day on the Hill I wandered into the Senate press gallery to see a scorching debate between Senators Javits and McClellan, the Arkansas Democrat who was chairman of the powerful Appropriations Committee. The issue was federal funds for education. Javits was a virtuoso at creating funding formulas that benefited New York, and McClellan was having none of it. As McClellan's face grew redder and redder, I took a seat, waiting for him to burst. Which he did. He pointed an accusing finger at Javits and said, "Mr. Javits, we don't need *your kind* in the United States Senate." He was not referring to Javits' party or state. He was referring to Javits' religion: Javits was a Jew. So much for the civility of yesteryear. Javits' staffers later told me that they would hear some southern senators who passed Javits in a Senate corridor mutter "Dirty Jew."

My wife had discovered Representative Ed Koch when he was a city councilman. He was invaluable in her research for her doctoral dissertation, on politics in New York City's police department. She urged me to befriend him. It didn't take much effort. Koch loved publicity, and owned one of the fastest mimeograph machines in town, forever spewing press releases. The New York delegation held frequent meetings, and Koch was the delegation's secretary. He would always give me a fill. His ceaseless publicity paid off: Koch went on to become a two-term mayor of New York City. New to Washington, I once asked Koch about a House-Senate conference in which neither body had approved funds for New York, but the conference nevertheless provided millions for the city. Koch explained: "With unanimous consent, they can make the sun rise in the west."

There was a great deal of intramural rivalry in the delegation. Representatives John Rooney and Hugh Carey, both Brooklyn Democrats and both Irish Catholics, hated each other. Rooney was instrumental in depriving Carey of ascending to the position of Majority Whip, which was ultimately filled by Thomas P. O'Neill, another Irish Catholic, from Massachusetts. Rooney, a power on the appropriations committee, told both President Kennedy and Speaker John McCormack that if they chose Carey for the spot, which usually led to the Speakership, he would block all federal appropriations to Massachusetts and all of Kennedy's legislative proposals.

Rooney was recovering from cancer surgery in April 1973, when I arrived in Washington, but I finally spied him in the Speaker's lobby, just off the House floor, where reporters could mingle with House members. I waited for Rooney to complete a conversation with some members and then walked up to him, introduced myself and said, "It's good to see you back here, Mr. Rooney." He gave me a typical Rooney response, addressing not me but other members. "Do they allow just anyone to come into the Speaker's lobby?" he asked, and then turned his back on me. What a sweetheart.

Another rivalry pitted Representative Mario Biaggi against Representative Jim Scheuer. Both were Bronx Democrats, fearful of being redistricted out of their seats after the next census. Each gave me material about the other. Scheuer's case against Biaggi was far more compelling. As a police officer, Biaggi was driving a police car chauffeuring two Mafioso when the car stopped at a traffic light. One of his passengers then murdered the other. Biaggi claimed he knew nothing about what had occurred and was given a medal for heroism.

There also was little love lost between Senators Javits and Abraham Ribicoff, a Connecticut Democrat. They were similar, the Senate's only Jews, both highly educated, both liberals. Ribicoff acted aloof, and I never understood why until I wrote a profile of him. After I interviewed him, I accompanied a photographer to his Watergate apartment and mentioned something I had just learned: Ribicoff had been born in a caul, a thin membrane that envelops a newborn. Cauls are rare, and folk cultures interpreted them as a sign of good fortune. A baby thus born was destined for greatness, or so it was believed. As a result, Ribicoff's parents sent him to both college and law school before his older brother, and indeed he walked and talked like a prince. When I mentioned the caul to Ribicoff, he asked if I'd like to see it. Indeed I did. The senator then mounted a step stool and retrieved a Garfinkel's department store box from one of his closets. He unwrapped tissue paper, and there stood a piece of what looked like dried up plastic. I told him I was amazed that he had kept it for 70-plus years and he explained that just as being born in a caul was a sign of great fortune, if that caul was ever harmed or destroyed, the opposite would occur: he would suffer irreversible bad fortune. Ribicoff said he wasn't superstitious, but wasn't taking any chances.

Although I initiated most of my articles, there was a major news event I also covered: the New York City fiscal crisis. After years, nay decades, of kicking the can down the road and giving city workers increased pensions and other benefits in lieu of large pay raises and using fiscal gimmicks like raiding the city's pension fund, the city finally had to pay the piper.

In the fall of 1975, with $453 million in debts come due and only $34 million in the bank, the city was virtually bankrupt. Since I was the reporter who covered Washington's impact on the New York City region, my assignment was to report on Washington's response to the city's bankruptcy. It wasn't pretty. In a speech that I covered at the National Press Club, President Gerald Ford vowed to veto any bill that provided money for a New York City bailout, resulting in a famous *New York Daily News* headline: "Ford to City: Drop Dead." Hugh Carey, denied a leadership role in Congress, had become governor of New York State. He agreed to give the city the necessary funds, provided that the city relinquish its authority to make financial decisions. To make those decisions, the city effectively surrendered its right to self-government. Carey appointed a Municipal Assistance Corporation, headed by Felix Rohatyn, a financier with Lazard Frere, a French investment house. The result: a wage freeze, tens of thousands of layoffs, increase in subway fare, tuition at previously free City University and hospital closings, among other austere measures. For my part, *The Times* often kept page one open until I had my nightly conversation with William Simon, the Treasury Secretary, who usually gave me enough information to fill a column. He never failed to call when I was on deadline, about 7:30 at night.

The senator overseeing New York's fiscal crisis was William Proxmire, a Wisconsin Democrat, chairman of the Banking Committee. He was one of the Senate's bona fide eccentrics. He never accepted campaign contributions, instead returning to Wisconsin every weekend, where he met with constituents. He also created what he called "Golden Fleece" awards, so named to draw attention to the fleecing of taxpayers. The awards singled out what he considered unneeded federal grants, many of them scientific, including a study of the sexual habits of bees. He was initially opposed to a New York City bailout, but eventually changed his mind. I was assigned to profile the senator for *The Times'* Sunday magazine. When I asked for an interview, his press secretary told me to be at his Ordway Street home 7:30 one morning. It was then I discovered that the senator jogged to his office in the Capitol, a distance of about six miles. To interview him, I had to jog alongside him, which I did. After several miles, I thought I'd die, but managed to keep pace with him until we reached the Capitol. I also interviewed his wife, Ellen, who had a catering business. She told me that the senator only briefly attended his own dinner parties. He didn't appear at the cocktail hour before the dinner and went to his study immediately after dinner, when his guests enjoyed after-dinner drinks. A day after my article was published, he called to invite us to dinner. He'd saved us a parking space outside his front door. When we arrived, he hurried out to escort us into the house, and stayed throughout the evening, when he escorted us back to our car. "What's this I read about your only briefly attending your own dinner parties?" I asked him. His response: "That shows how much you can rely on what you read in the papers." The senator eventually supported a New York City bailout, instrumental in getting the city several billion dollars of federal money.

The New York City fiscal crisis gave me one of my most frustrating experiences at *The Times*. I had arranged an interview with Roderick Hills, chairman of the Securities and Exchange Commission, who gave me what I considered a great story: the great brokerage houses, including Felix Rohatyn's Lazard Frere, had anticipated the city's bankruptcy and had sold their own holdings of municipal bonds before the crisis. But they had not told their customers, who continued to purchase New York City paper. By chance, a *Times* reporter was a weekend guest at Rohatyn's vacation home, and *The Times* sent him my article for comment from Rohatyn, who vehemently denied it. *The Times* delayed publication of my article for several days and finally ran it on a Sunday, in the back pages. How could *The Times* have given the same weight to a participant as they gave to the chairman of the commission that regulates his industry? The story deserved better.

After three years as *The Times*' regional reporter in Washington, reporting on New York, New Jersey and Connecticut, a job I thoroughly enjoyed, my canvas was about to become much larger.

5

A BROADER CANVAS

In January 1977, Dave Jones, who succeeded Gene Roberts as national editor, promoted me to congressional correspondent. It was a promotion I had sought because, much as I had enjoyed covering the New York, New Jersey and Connecticut delegations, my new assignment provided a broader canvas. Now I would report on the entire Congress. I also would formally be part of the Washington bureau, instead of a Metro desk outpost. My predecessors as regional reporters had been given an office to themselves, isolated from the rest of the bureau. I had sought, and been given, a desk in the middle of the newsroom, but I was still considered an alien.

Like the newsroom in New York, the Washington bureau also had its share of eccentrics. Good reporters can be hard to take, and *The Times*' Washington bureau was no exception. The best reporters—Seymour Hersh, David Burnham, Charlie Mohr, Jim Naughton, Phil Shabecoff, Jim Wooten—could be difficult. Robert Pear was an exception, an extremely soft-spoken man who knew more about health care than almost anyone. Sy Hersh had broken the My Lai massacre story, as well as the story of torture of Iraqi POWS. In the Washington bureau, I often saw and heard him on the phone screaming at a bureaucrat.

I found Congress fascinating, and I still get a lump in my throat at the sight of the Capitol's large white dome. Under that dome were clashing ambitions, fiery rhetoric, and deals made and broken. The members of Congress could not hide their ambition. Many House members wanted to be governors or senators, and most senators saw themselves as future presidents. They walked a tightrope, seeking to please two constituencies, the folks back home and the party leadership, which placed them on committees, and determined which bills would reach the floor. Their ambition was revealed in every vote and statement, both by what was said and what was left unsaid. Most had few friends among their colleagues, or even back home. It had taken total concentration on their careers to achieve their status, with little time or energy to develop true friendships.

Five Myths About Congress

I received a political education reporting on the Hill and quickly learned to disregard conventional wisdom, including:

1. "This is the most polarized Congress in history." Hardly. It's hard to believe, in this day and age when there are so few moderates in Congress and such reluctance to compromise, but things have been a lot worse. Since I began reporting on Congress, many political experts have bemoaned what they regarded as its polarization. Every Congress was called the most polarized in history. In fact, no latter day Congress could compare in polarity with the enmity that existed during the Civil Rights battles on the Hill, which pitted northern members vs. southerners, or with the Vietnam War battles that divided hawks and doves.

2. "There were giants in those days." Many observers look back longingly at what they considered the congressional giants of the past. In fact, when I came to Washington in 1973, both the House and Senate were ruled by southerners. In the one-party south, they easily gained seniority by winning election after election. Most were bigoted reactionaries. Sen Richard Russell is often cited as one of the giants in the past. A Georgia Democrat, he even has a Senate office building named after him. He was chairman of the Appropriations committee, a highly educated,

erudite man with excellent manners. He also was a racist and reactionary. Other racist–reactionary southerners who ruled the roost included James Eastland (D–Miss.), chairman of the Judiciary Committee; Strom Thurmond (D–Miss.), chairman of Armed Services committee; Jesse Helms (D–N.C.), chairman of Foreign Relations committee; John McClellan (D–Ark.), chairman of the Government Operations committee; Eugene Talmadge (D–Ga.), chairman of the Agriculture committee. In the House, Howard Smith (D–Va.), chairman of the Rules committee, single–handedly blocked civil rights legislation from reaching the House floor, while John Rankin (D–Miss.) railed against blacks and Jews, calling Albert Einstein a communist agitator.

3. "Congress was more democratic in the old days." Just the opposite. Because of the iron–rule of southerners, freshman senators had to wait their turn, sometimes years, before making a speech on the floor, or introducing a bill. Today, chairmanships are distributed more diversely. House and Senate rules ban legislators from having more than one chairmanship of an important committee, or a committee chairmanship and subcommittee chairmanship of lesser committees. In addition, television enables legislators to speak directly to their constituents.

4. "Congress is isolated behind all that marble on the Hill." Few Americans are less isolated. Most legislators return home every weekend, to attend Town Halls, weddings, bar mitzvahs and other events. Their survival depends on their knowledge of their district and the approval of their constituents. Hence, Tip O'Neill's dictum, "All politics is local." Congress is a fairly accurate representative of the American people. When the nation is deadlocked, Congress is deadlocked. When the American people want action, Congress acts. In addition, anything that happens anywhere in the world intersects the Congress. Legislators must react swiftly to major events wherever they occur.

5. "You can't defeat a million dollars." You sure can. Experience, incumbency, integrity, respect of voters and political smarts are potent political assets. The saying that "money is the mother's milk of politics" is true, but an abundance of money doesn't offset those lacking these assets. Donald Trump won the presidency despite spending $500 million less than Hillary Clinton's

$1.2 billion, and indeed, less than any presidential candidate since John McCain in 2008. Many zillionaires have gone down to defeat, including Michael Huffington, who spent $28 million in an unsuccessful campaign against Senator Dianne Feinstein, a California Democrat who spent $4 million. Linda McMahon, the professional wrestling mogul, spent $100 million on two unsuccessful Senate races in Connecticut.

I began my reporting of Congress by introducing myself to the party leaders and requesting interviews. Senator Robert Byrd of West Virginia, the Democratic leader, was the first to respond. Byrd had belonged to the Ku Klux Klan in his young adulthood. Without this membership, he was unlikely to achieve political success in his home town of Sophia and environs, then advance to the West Virginia House of Delegates, state Senate, U.S. House of Representatives and the U.S. Senate, where he served for 46 years, the longest serving senator in history. In much the same way, Barack Obama's membership in the Trinity United Church, led by Rev. Jeremiah Wright, a radical firebrand, was a necessary marker for Obama's political success in the Chicago ghetto, and his ascendance to the state Senate, U.S. Senate and presidency. Once firmly launched on their political careers, Byrd rejected the KKK, and Obama rejected Rev. Wright.

Hedrick Smith, then *The Times*' Washington bureau chief, accompanied me to the Byrd interview, in the senator's opulent office. I began with my tape recorder on, and Byrd was taciturn. After about 45 minutes, Smith had to leave and my tape had expired. That's when Byrd opened up. Byrd's mother had died in childbirth, in North Carolina, and he was raised by her sister and brother-in-law in West Virginia. Born Cornelius Calvin Sales Jr., he changed his name to that of the couple who had raised him. Byrd recalled that his adoptive father was an impoverished coal miner. A customary Christmas present was an orange in Byrd's Christmas stocking. One year they came into a bit of money, and his Christmas present was a tricycle that he kept in his Arlington, Va., apartment until the end of his days.

His adoptive parents also were emotionally impoverished. "I have no recollection of having been kissed as a child," Byrd told me, in what *The Times* selected as the Quote of the Day. Even as Byrd advanced politically, his adoptive parents kept their distance. But after his election as senator, he received a letter from his adoptive father, who wanted to see him. They spent a week together in Sophia. "That was many years ago," Byrd recalled, "and the last time I saw him." I said that must have been some week they spent together. No, Byrd said, the week was uneventful, but just as his adoptive father had no desire to see him when he grew up, Byrd now had no further desire to see his adoptive father.

As a senator, Byrd chose his words with great care. Sometimes he would hesitate for several minutes before answering a question. One could almost see the wheels of his mind pondering different answers before settling on the one he thought best. A conservative Democrat, he slowly became more moderate, and said his votes against the civil rights bills were the ones he most regretted. The Senate was Byrd's home, and he was a master of its rules. He met with reporters Saturday mornings, making me work six days a week. We sat around his large conference table, and Byrd answered any questions we might have. I often brought my kids to Byrd's sessions. They sat in chairs behind the reporters. I wanted them to see what my job was like.

In a more relaxed manner, James A. Baker, an ultra-smooth and sophisticated Texan who was President Reagan's chief-of-staff, also met with reporters on Saturdays, no appointment required. But Baker's sessions were one-on-one. Like Byrd, he also answered any questions we might have. I found him especially helpful in setting up interviews with President Reagan.

My last interview with Reagan occurred late in his second term. I was doing a magazine article about Al D'Amato's challenge to Jacob Javits, a sitting senator, in a New York primary. I asked the president how he felt about it. "That's an odd one," he said. I asked the question a different way. Same answer. I asked it a third way. Same answer. I then went on to other questions. Same answer. I ended the interview after about 15 minutes, whereupon Reagan took me on a 30-minute tour of the Oval Office, pointing out where he had received various memorabilia. I didn't think about it. I thought Reagan was just being cagey. But now I think it was the beginning of his dementia.

My next interview was with Thomas P. "Tip" O'Neill Jr. Unlike Byrd, Tip was a natural politician. To him, all women were "darlin'" and in need of a kiss. All men were pals, especially when he couldn't recall their names. "How ya doin', pal?" he would ask. Carl Albert

PHOTO 5.1 President Ronald Reagan. Extremely congenial, he seldom gave me useful information, but spent time giving me tours of his memorabilia in the Oval Office. (White House photo)

was Speaker, but too fond of the grape, and Tip, Majority leader when I arrived, was the power behind the throne. He then became Speaker.

Tip had a fount of stories. One of his favorites was about a freshman from Michigan who arrived on the Hill the same year he did, in 1953. Tip took John F. Kennedy's seat when the future president was elected to the Senate. The Michigan legislator confided to Tip that he was the target of a Justice Department investigation of alleged tax evasion. He didn't know if they were considering a civil or criminal case against him, and the case had been going on for years. Tip advised the Michigander to talk to Sam Rayburn, the legendary, long-time Speaker. "It's like water torture," the Michigander told Rayburn. "It's drip, drip, drip." Rayburn told him to return to the Speaker's office at 6 p.m. The Speaker then called the Attorney General and

PHOTO 5.2 Speaker Thomas P. "Tip" O'Neill. I became much too close to Tip, with whom Charlie and I golfed. He was very angry when I wrote a critical story and didn't speak to me for exactly one year. (Author's photo)

said he wanted a decision on the congressman's case no later than 6 p.m. When the congressman returned, Rayburn told him that the Justice department was considering only a civil case, not a criminal one. The congressman was practically in tears. "I want you to know that anytime you need my vote, it's yours," he told Rayburn.

"Funny you should say that," the Speaker said. "We have an offshore oil bill coming up Monday, and I need your vote." "You've got it," the congressman said. But when he returned to his district, the local newspaper published a story that he had sold his vote on offshore oil in exchange for getting off the hook on income tax evasion charges. An incensed bureaucrat at the Justice Department had probably contacted his local newspaper.

When he returned to the Capitol he went to the Speaker's office and told Rayburn he had a problem. He then told him about the newspaper article, and said if he voted with Rayburn on offshore oil, he'd probably have the shortest term on record. "You promised me your vote," Rayburn told him, "and I expect you to keep your promise. I want you to sit in one of the first few rows during the voting, and if I need your vote, I'll signal you. If I don't need your vote, you may vote as you please." The congressman did as he was told, sweating bullets until the last minutes of the voting, when Rayburn signaled that he didn't need his vote. The congressman heaved a huge sigh of relief, and saw a dozen other congressmen in the first few rows also heaving a huge sigh of relief. "If you want to know how this place was run in the old days, that's how," O'Neill said.

In the ensuing years I became close to Tip, probably too close for a reporter. We vacationed in Wellfleet and he had a summer home in nearby Harwich. He was the first Catholic to be admitted to "Eastward Ho," a beautiful golf course on a peninsula in Chatham. Most fairways had views of the sea. But Tip was shunned by the other members, who declined to golf with him. It was the old "No Irish Need Apply" attitude of the Boston bluebloods. Possibly in desperation, Tip would call us, and ask if my son Charlie would like to play golf the following day. Charlie was always delighted. Then he would ask if I would like to join him and Charlie. We loved playing golf with Tip, who had a very good game. He would smoke his cigar and tell stories between golf shots. We also played in Washington, stealing away on sunny afternoons to play at Haines Point, a public course. We were often teamed up with other players, who seldom realized they were playing golf with the Speaker. Tip always introduced himself as Tom.

That's why Tip was stung when I wrote an article about how he had intervened on behalf of a Rochester developer who also was finance chairman of the Democratic Party. The developer had built a high-rise apartment house that he intended to sell as condos but lacked sufficient customers. He then changed them to rental units, but failed there as well. Finally, in desperation, he applied to the Department of Housing and Urban Development for subsidies for low income tenants. I received a call from a rival real estate builder, who said that Tip was lobbying Carla Hills, the HUD secretary, on his friend's behalf. I called Tip's press secretary for comment and a few hours later was told that Tip had never intervened on behalf of the developer. I then called Carla Hills, who said, "He's always calling," and promised to call back with a list of Tip's calls, which she did. "Tip called May 9 at 2:30 and asked, 'What's happening with those subsidies?'" He called June 12 at 10:30, June 25th at 4:18, July 3d at 5:42, and so on.

Tip didn't talk to me for a year after my article appeared. Then, exactly a year to the day later, he gave me an interview. At the end he leaned back in his chair and said, "You know, Marty, I'm Irish and we Irish never carry grudges." I replied: "The thought never occurred to me, Mr. Speaker." Tip then said, "But that article you wrote was such a piece of shit." After that we were back on track.

I made a habit of popping into Tip's office late in the afternoon and just kibitzing. At one point I was writing a profile of Jim Wright, the Majority leader, and I asked, "When are you going to let Jim sit in this chair?" His response was swift: "That shows what you know," he said. "Next term will be my last one. All I want is to be ambassador to Ireland." I didn't take a note, but after I left his office I immediately called the desk and was told to write the story about his forthcoming retirement. At 6:30 *The Times* sent George Tames, a great photographer, to take a portrait of Tip, and then I got a call from Chris Matthews, Tip's press secretary, who had gone home. "What's going on?" he asked. "Nothing special," I said. "They just wanted an updated photo." Chris threatened, "If you're lying to me, I'll never talk to you again," he said. The story occupied a good portion of page one in the next day's paper. I had beaten *The Boston Globe* on a major political story on its own turf. In his biography, *Man of the House*, Tip wrote that his wife, Millie, chewed him out by saying, "You always said, 'All politics is local,' and then you give your retirement story to the *New York Times*."

Bob Michel of Peoria, Ill., the House Republican leader, was a moderate in every way, politically and personally. He had a beautiful voice and would sing duets with Tip at social gatherings. He and Tip maintained a solid friendship. The two would occasionally sneak away during the day and play golf at a local course. This all was grist for Newt Gingrich, who ousted Michel as Republican leader and would become a confrontational Speaker.

Howard H. Baker Jr., of Tennessee, the Senate Republican leader, was an amateur photographer. He was seldom without his camera and would photograph meetings in his office, and events in and around the Capitol, including cabinet meetings. Like the other leaders, every morning before a congressional session he invited reporters onto the Senate floor and briefed them about the day's schedule. Alas, Baker's briefings were often obfuscated. Fortunately, he had an aide, Tom Griscom, a former Tennessee reporter whom the state legislature affectionately designated as "the state insect," to follow Baker's briefings and explain what the senator really meant. Low key and often rumpled, Baker was a skilled negotiator. James Baker III, President Reagan's chief-of-staff and Secretary of the Treasury, described him as "the quintessential mediator, negotiator and moderator." Senator Baker was best known for his question during the Senate investigation of Watergate: "What did the President (Nixon) know, and when did he know it?" Later in life he married another Republican senator, Nancy Kassebaum of Kansas, the daughter of Alf Landon, the Republican who had run against FDR in 1936. Howard Baker later became chief-of-staff of the Reagan White House. One of the highlights of my congressional career was writing a magazine profile of Senator Baker, for which I won the Everett M. Dirksen Award for Distinguished Reporting of Congress.

Barely a year after reporting on the Congress, I was sent to the White House to report on the presidency of Jimmy Carter. The Carter folks had been unhappy with Charlie Mohr and Jim Wooten, two experienced reporters who were models of journalistic rectitude. Nevertheless, the Carter people wrongly thought they were biased against them, and they were ultimately replaced by Terry Smith and me. Terry grew up in the newspaper business. His father, Red Smith, was a premier sports columnist, first with the *New York Herald Tribune* and later *The New York Times*. Terry was a very good writer who later went on to work for CBS. At a lunch at a fancy French restaurant, Wooten warned me, "Don't cheapen the beat." Translation: continue to dine at very good, somewhat expensive restaurants.

Our first week at the White House, Zbigniew Brzezinski, Carter's national security advisor, invited Terry and me to a foreign policy briefing in his office. It began in late afternoon, in bright daylight, and continued for about 90 minutes. When we emerged, it was totally dark. A map of the world covered most of a wall, and Brzezinski went over all the trouble spots. He then told us that there would

Best wishes to Marty Tolchin —
Jimmy Carter

PHOTO 5.3 President Jimmy Carter. I interviewed him only a few times. He was very wary of the media. Terry Smith, my White House partner, is on the left. (White House photo)

be times when we had most of a story but lacked a key piece of the puzzle. When that happened, he told us, call him directly, not Jerry Schecter, his press secretary, and he would help us when he could. Which he did.

As it happened, foreign policy became a very important part of our beat. President Carter was determined to achieve peace between Israelis and Palestinians, and invited Both Israel's Prime Minister Menachem Begin and Egyptian President Anwar Sadat to Camp David, the presidential woodland retreat in the Catoctin mountains. Unfortunately, *The Times* was not publishing, because of a printer's strike. My friend Bill Safire had been asked by New York's public television station to go to New York several times a week and comment on the talks. He declined, but referred them to me. I made the trip twice a week, and recorded two or three tapes each time. It gave me great respect for television reporters, who have to boil most stories down to under two minutes. Finally, Begin and Sadat signed the Camp David Accords. These mortal enemies even shook hands. It was Carter's greatest success as president. The accords provided a framework for peace in the Middle East, and led directly to the treaty between Egypt and Israel.

Despite this enormous achievement, the Carter White House was totally disorganized. Jody Powell, the press secretary, would cancel news conferences several times a day. Hamilton Jordan, chief-of-staff, had refused Tip O'Neill extra tickets to the inauguration gala, which Tip ultimately received. How do you refuse the Speaker of the House of Representatives? Thereafter, Tip referred to Hamilton Jordan as Hannibal Jerkin.

The president himself was a micromanager, down to determining who could play on the White House tennis courts, hardly something with which a president should be concerned. A policy announced in the morning would be rescinded in the afternoon and reinstated in the evening.

Like every White House, the Carter White House had only a few designated leakers. In addition to Brzezinski on foreign policy, Stuart Eizenstat, the chief domestic policy advisor, also could be helpful. But mostly, the way to report on the White House was to go outside the White House fence. The Hill was the repository of a great deal of White House information, and, as always, leaked like a sieve. The Chamber of Commerce and labor unions also could be helpful. My problem was getting back to the White House for often delayed news conferences.

Early in my White House days, I inadvertently embarrassed Eizenstat. He recalls in his biography of President Carter:

> I made a rookie mistake during the transition of telling *New York Times* reporter Martin Tolchin that our legislative agenda would be "modest," remembering President Kennedy's adage that great initiatives cannot be built on slim electoral margins—earning me one of Carter's only personal rebukes. In fact, at his direction, we launched a veritable blizzard of "comprehensive" domestic reforms.

> (*President Carter, The White House Years*, St. Martin's Press, 2018, p. 68)

In 1980, as a poorly masqueraded campaign strategy, Carter decided to take the Delta Queen, an old-fashioned sternwheeler, down the Mississippi, from St. Paul to St. Louis. Stops included Iowa, Kansas and Nebraska. The reporters' bedroom was somewhat primitive, with rainwater pouring into the center of the room. We placed our beds in a star, so that the tips of the beds avoided the water. When the reporters asked the president if he could keep in touch with the rest of the world floating down the river on the Delta Queen, we were informed that White House communications could handle the president's needs anywhere in the world. The president was so bored with the trip that he called in reporters for a drink before dinner.

At the same time I was going down the Mississippi, my wife Susan and a woman colleague were in Lagos, at the invitation of the Nigerian government, to give a brief course in public administration to government officials. Alas, the government was mediating a local war, and she was advised that there was a Chad warrior sleeping in what should have been her bed. She did what all red-blooded Americans do in such a situation, and called the ambassador, who invited her to stay in his residence, which she did. She then tried to communicate this in messages to me aboard the Delta Queen. The first message finally reached me three days later. Quite a commentary on White House communications.

I also reported on Walter Mondale, a liberal Minnesota Democrat who was Carter's vice president. Mondale was beloved by reporters for taking up the cause of education and the arts, but he was one of the last senators who were silent on the Vietnam War. In a magazine profile, I called him a "professional protégé" because he took his orders from the senior senator Hubert Humphrey, who was slow to oppose the war.

After two years, I was tired of covering the White House, and asked to go back to covering Congress. After a few months, my wish was granted.

One of my most interesting reporting assignments was the Iran Contra investigation. President Reagan had authorized the sale of weapons from Israel to Iran, whose money then went to the Nicaraguan contras. Israel would then be resupplied. This was in violation of the Boland amendment, which banned all aid to the contras. I had a source on the Senate investigation committee. I would meet him in

PHOTO 5.4 Walter F. Mondale, a liberal Minnesota Democrat who was Carter's vice president. He was unhappy with my description of him as a "professional protégé" for taking orders from his senior Democrat, Hubert Humphrey, who was late in opposing the Vietnam War and resorted to underhanded methods to defeat a Republican running for governor. (White House photo)

his office after the day's session. Cautious about divulging information he had sworn to keep secret, the senator spoke in riddles. "The jackal yelps, but the caravan moves on," he might say. Was I correct in assuming the jackal was Col. Oliver North? Was the caravan the White House? In a few cryptic sentences, I had my story.

I also reported on many budget negotiations. Although the articles appeared on page one, few people actually read them. On several occasions, my mother, an avid *Times* reader, would call and ask if everything was okay because she hadn't seen me in the paper recently. I often told her to look at page one. Once, at about 2 in the morning, covering a budget negotiation, I called in my story. The national desk copy editor advised that my article would only appear in the relatively few papers distributed at the Times Square kiosks.

"Even as we speak," she said, "ladies of the evening are gathering at the kiosks to learn if the deficit was increased by 3/8ths of a percent or 5/8ths."

About this time, Sue and I invited Senator James Sasser (D-Tenn.) to a dinner party at our home, where he told us that Nissan had opened a factory in Smyrna, Tenn., and that Nissan executives were supporting his Republican opponent, Representative Robin Beard. This was a new development in American politics, the intrusion of a foreign company's executives into American elections. I went to Smyrna to check it out. I saw signs throughout the factory supporting Beard. The issue was domestic content, which Sasser supported and Beard opposed. The bill required a percentage of every foreign car made to be manufactured in the U.S. to avoid import taxes. I had lunch with the Nissan executives, who were all Americans, who said they were merely expressing their right of free speech. I asked them if they had checked with Tokyo before taking a position on the election. "We check everything we do with Tokyo," they said. I had my story, which led to a book, *Buying Into America: How Foreign Investment Is Changing the Nation*. The book described how states vied with each other with incentives including tax breaks to woo foreign investors. Lester Thurow, dean of MIT's School of Management, reviewed the book for *The Times*, and wrote that the book was "must reading for every state legislator and governor in the country." It was the best seller among all our books, and the only book in the window of a Washington bookstore that specialized in books dealing with economics and finance.

During this period I was elected shop steward in the Washington bureau. No one else wanted the job, which consisted largely of representing colleagues out of favor with management, sometimes justifiably, and participating in labor negotiations. My philosophy was non-confrontational. I thought that both union and management had the same goal: a successful *New York Times*. I got this from a dear friend, Steve Schlossberg, who was longtime counsel to the United Auto Workers., whose executives were actually on the board of General Motors. President Reagan later appointed Steve U.S. representative to the International Labor Organization, in Geneva. Steve's wife, Nancy, was a distinguished professor at the University of Maryland.

I always maintained that there's no such thing as a lazy employee. Everyone wants to be productive. Nobody gets up in the morning and says, "How can I waste another day of my life?" If someone isn't productive, it's up to management to find out why. Remember, it was management that hired them in the first place. I later learned that some employees are, in fact, hopeless. At *The Hill* there was an advertising salesman who padded his expense account, including phantom trips across the country, and phantom dinners with his clients. I had to let him go, without the bonuses he had earned, which were less than the money he had taken.

As shop steward, I also was involved in collective bargaining, which I enjoyed immensely. At one point I began to believe that almost everyone at the negotiating table had a vested interest in *not* resolving disputes. Both sides wanted to show how tough they were.

I was directly involved in settling two disputes. In one case, management offered a buyout to senior employees, usually those with the highest salaries. The Newspaper Guild was in the awful position of opposing the buyouts, on the grounds that the company wasn't putting enough money into the pension and health benefit plans to cover the cost of the buyouts. Management insisted they were. Because of the stalemate, management had to let go the most recent hires, usual women and minorities.

I back-channeled, and called the publisher, Arthur Sulzberger Jr. I said, "Arthur, you're not an actuary and I'm not an actuary. Why don't we get an actuary, or two actuaries, one appointed by management and the other by the Guild. If they say you're putting enough money in, that's okay with us, and if they say you need to put more money in, you'll do so." Arthur readily agreed, and so did the union president. But Arthur wanted me to clear this with *The Times* company's president. I said, "Arthur, I don't deal with underlings." Arthur said, "For God's sake, Marty, he's the president of the Times company."

So I went to New York to meet with *The Times* company's president, Lance Primus. But before I did, I sought the advice of my friend Steve Schlossberg, as well as Lane Kirkland, then president of the AFL–CIO, and Sol Linowitz, who negotiated the Panama Canal treaty. They all gave me the same advice: be prepared for a harangue on how the unions are destroying newspapers, and come up with

PHOTO 5.5 Arthur Ochs Sulzberger Jr., *The Times'* publisher with whom I back-channeled to end two deadlocked labor disputes. ([Damon Winter] Copyright 2017 *The New York Times*)

three separate plans. They were right on both counts. The day after my meeting with Primus, Sue and I were off to Bellagio, Italy, to spend a month at the Rockefeller Foundation villa and begin a new book. The first telephone call came from the union president, saying that they had agreed to one of my plans. The second came from *The Times* publisher, thanking me for my work in putting the compromise together.

Another dispute involved contract negotiations. The union's contract with *The Times* had expired, and the negotiators were not even talking to each other. Again, I called Sulzberger with a proposal. I asked him to designate four or five management negotiators and the Guild would do the same. We then would go out to several dinners, with absolutely no discussion involving the negotiations. We could talk about anything else: our kids, sports, movies, anything but the negotiations. The Guild hosted the first dinner, and I selected the Lotos Club in New York, a beautiful venue with wonderful food. I had reciprocity through the University Club in

Washington, where I swam. Management hosted the second dinner, at a swanky Italian restaurant in mid-town. After these two dinners, the negotiators began to see their opposites as human beings. They returned to the bargaining table, and a new contract was ironed out fairly quickly.

As shop steward, it also was my responsibility to represent *Times* employees out of favor with management. In addition, I continued my policy of giving management a heads-up when there was resentment over a *Times* policy. One bureau chief did not appreciate this effort. When he asked a number of reporters to check out porno stores to see if they could find films rented or purchased by Clarence Thomas, during his hearing to be a Supreme Court justice, a number of reporters came to me and asked me to convey their resentment. Checking out porno films was not why they had joined *The New York Times*. "Are you here in an official capacity?" the bureau chief asked me. "No, I'm here as a colleague, giving you a heads up," I replied. "Marty, you're not part of management and I'm not interested in anything you have to say in your unofficial capacity," the bureau chief responded. I left his office, a bit shaken, and asked the copy desk to carefully check the story I was in the middle of writing. As was my custom, I relayed this experience to my wife and kids at the dinner table. After dinner, the telephone rang. Charlie answered the phone and told me it was the bureau chief, who apologized for his behavior.

During the Thomas hearings, I received a tip involving Senator Howard Metzenbaum (D-Ohio). I was told that his top judiciary committee staffer had discouraged a black law professor from testifying on Thomas' behalf. The White House had searched for a black law professor to provide such testimony, and found one at the University of Washington law school. He checked into the Willard hotel. His expertise was in real estate law. The Metzenbaum staffer had visited him in his hotel room, and told him that if he testified, her boss would focus on his ignorance of constitutional law, and humiliate him. The professor packed his bags and flew home the next morning, without testifying. I went to her office, but she wasn't there. I went back to the bureau, and called Metzenbaum. "Do you want Clarence Thomas on the Supreme Court?" he asked. I told him my personal views were irrelevant. "You're going to destroy this woman," he said.

In fact, after being reprimanded by the Senate Ethics committee, she left her job and wound up at Georgetown University law school, where she has taught for decades.

Although I tried to avoid getting involved with policy, I played a very minor role in enactment of the Simpson-Mazzoli immigration bill of 1986. One day I ran into Senator Alan Simpson, a lanky Wyoming Republican with a fabulous sense of humor, on the Capitol Plaza. He was cursing Tip O'Neill. What was the problem? The Senate had passed the Simpson-Mazzoli bill, and O'Neill blocked it from coming to the House floor. "Do you know Tip?" I asked. He did not. "Let me introduce you to him." I led him to Tip's office, introduced the two and voila, Tip changed his mind and allowed a House vote. President Reagan signed the bill, and it became law.

Abe Rosenthal, *The Times'* executive editor, always feared what he considered the leftward drift of the newspaper. He chided a moderate-left Washington bureau chief as a "communist." Neil Lewis recalled a dinner meeting to which Abe invited the entire Washington bureau, perhaps 50 reporters and editors. Abe asked for a show of hands of those who considered themselves liberals. An overwhelming number of hands shot up. Then he asked for a similar display from those who considered themselves conservatives. Two hands were airborne. Abe exulted that this demonstrated the imbalance that he had feared. John Herbers, a soft-spoken southerner, raised his hand and said something like, "Abe I think what you just did was highly improper. It's just not appropriate for an editor to ask his staff about their political leanings." Abe seemed stunned. At the time, Abe was at the height of his authority and was known to make people pay for displeasing him, Lewis recalled. "So we all tensed up wondering how he would respond. After a long pause, Abe said, 'You know, you're right. I apologize.' We were astonished." A few years later, Herbers was promoted to news editor in the bureau.

I enjoyed investigative reporting, never more so than in the case of Michael Deaver, who had been a top lieutenant of President Reagan. I got a tip that five months after Deaver retired from his White House job, he had been lobbying his former colleagues on behalf of South Korea. As part of my investigation, I was joined by Stuart Diamond, an excellent reporter, in traveling to Seoul to determine the truth of this allegation. It was not that difficult to do. After our article was published, Representative John Dingell, a Michigan Democrat who was chairman of a powerful oversight committee, asked Deaver to testify about our report, which he totally denied. Dingell thought he was lying and referred Deaver's denial to the Justice Department. In 1987, Deaver was convicted of perjury and sentenced to three years' probation.

On two occasions I ran afoul of *The Times* management. In one case I gave a blurb to a book written by Jim Wright, who had finally become Speaker. The book turned out to be a vehicle to circumvent the rules limiting campaign funds and expenditures. Wright's supporters purchased cartons of the books, in an effort to swell his campaign coffer. *The Times* then forbade its reporters from giving book blurbs. In his memoir, Max Frankel wrote that I had "thoughtlessly" given the blurb. Not so. In fact, I had asked the bureau chief's permission to do so, and we had several discussions on the matter. Most reporters were thrilled by the new *Times* order. How do you resist giving a blurb requested by the Speaker when you're reporting on Congress? *The Times* made it easy.

The second occasion was when I wrote an article for the *Sunday Review* about foreign investments, the subject of one of my books. I pointed out that those investments frequently brought foreign companies into our political system. The article was denounced by Senator Steve Syms, an Idaho Republican, in a speech on the Senate floor. Frankel was unhappy. Why was a senator unhappy with the article? Of course, it's not a reporter's purpose to please politicians, but Frankel was upset and ordered an investigation. To the best of my knowledge, nothing came of it.

At about this time, Arthur Gelb, then managing editor, who had become a good friend, said he'd like to have dinner with a few reporters who had worked for him when he was Metro editor. I asked him to send me a list of invitees. He did. There were about 50 names on the list. Arthur wanted it billed as a non-retirement dinner, which did not exactly fit the facts. Arthur was about to retire as managing editor and assume a new position as head of the NYTimes Foundation. I decided to hold the dinner in the private, upstairs dining room at Sardi's. I sent out invitations that said that they should RSVP by sending me a check. All but one did. About two weeks before the dinner,

The Times' food critic wrote a scathing review of the food and service at Sardi's. I was flooded with phone calls asking me to change the venue, but it was too late. Actually, the food and service were great, as every owner and manager appeared at the dinner, standing behind the diners, one for every two reporters. The best part of the dinner was the reminiscences. I told my Shea Stadium story. There were many great stories. Gay Talese said that *The Times* years were the happiest of his life. Because of the job? "Because I was young," he said. Someone told a story about Ada Louise Huxtable, *The Times'* diminutive architecture critic. Every week, Arthur had lunch with all *The Times* critics. At one such lunch, they were all lobbying to be able to use a four letter word for sex. Arthur adamantly refused. After the lunch, Arthur and Ada Louise got into the same elevator, to return to the newsroom. Ada Louise kept up the pressure. "Arthur, we have to be able to use that word," she said. "What word is that?" Arthur asked. "You know, the word we've been talking about during the whole lunch." Ada Louise replied. Arthur said, "Ada Louise, you can't even use that word in a crowded elevator, and you want me to put it on page one of the *New York Times*?"

I created my last three assignments at *The Times*. The first was a series on judicial activism. Increasingly, judges were running school districts, state hospitals and prisons. For my first interview I went to Alabama and saw Judge Frank Johnson, a federal judge who was running the state's prisons and mental hospitals. I also interviewed Governor George Wallace, who had been a close friend of Johnson's. In fact, Johnson ran Wallace's successful campaign for president of the student body at the University of Alabama. Wallace told me that he was not that displeased with Johnson's role, and said that Johnson was doing things that Wallace couldn't do for political reasons. He had come a long way from "Segregation Today, Segregation tomorrow, Segregation forever." Perhaps being shot during his presidential campaign and living his life in a wheelchair gave him more sympathy for underdogs.

I also interviewed David Bazelon, chief judge of the Federal Court of Appeals in the District of Columbia. We had met socially, and he agreed to be interviewed. "What time should I arrive at your office?" I asked. Bazelon: "I don't want to do it in my office." Me: "What's your favorite restaurant?" Bazelon: "I don't want to do it in a restaurant." Me: "Where would you like to do it?" Bazelon: "Have your wife invite me and my wife for dinner, and if the dinner is good, we'll do it at your home." And so we did. The Bazelons were immediately charmed by our children, Charlie and Karen, and took them to movies, plays, the circus and restaurants. We became very good friends.

The other assignment I created for myself was a series on the increased use of privatization. Financially strapped states and cities farmed out services they previously provided, at much less cost because the private companies didn't have to pay the employee benefits paid by these governments. I had a problem with private prisons run by companies including Behavior Modification Inc. I thought that such deprivation of an individual's liberty should be performed by government, not private companies.

Finally, several friends who had clients halfway around the world told me that, for the first time, they were getting sick after flights back from Asia, Africa and the Middle East. I called Boeing and asked their public relations representatives if there was any explanation. I was put in touch with the company's engineers, who suggested that it might have something to do with a change the airlines had requested, which gave pilots the ability to reduce the amount of fresh air coming into the cabins. The air comes in at very cold temperatures, and is warmed by the aircraft engines. With 100% fresh air, the cost to an airline is roughly $100,000 per plane annually. The major airlines have tens of thousands of planes. But the cost is significantly reduced when the air is re-circulated, which the airlines now do. My article led to a lawsuit by flight attendants, some of whom had gotten tuberculosis, which they attributed to the re-circulated air. They lost the lawsuit.

Nevertheless, *The Times* was and remains the world's greatest newspaper, and it was an honor to work there, alongside the greatest journalists in the business. I had assumed that after my retirement, the quality of *The Times* would plummet. Instead, it has soared. Its coverage of the presidency of Donald Trump has sharpened the paper, which now has far more investigative articles than in my day, when many editors were reluctant to rock the boat. Although still cautious about what gets into print, editors have given reporters far more leeway in developing their articles. *The Times'* editorials have more bite, and the opinion pages more relevance. It has more foreign correspondents than any other news organization, and its coverage of finance, science, the arts and other subjects remains top flight. If you want to know what will be on the evening news, read *The Times* in the morning.

6

THE HILL AND *POLITICO*

In December 1993, I was visited by Jerry Finkelstein, a New York City mogul who, among other things, owned two dozen weekly newspapers. He wanted to buy *Roll Call*, a 40-year-old newspaper that reported on Capitol Hill but considered the asking price, $14.5 million, too high. He wanted me to start another weekly Capitol Hill newspaper.

I was happy at *The Times*. After nearly 40 years, I was finally getting the hang of it. I knew how the paper worked and had friends in most editorial departments. They had taken care of me during newspaper strikes, giving me magazine and other free-lance assignments. I had no desire to leave. So I sent him away. Jerry is nothing if not persistent, however, and returned three more times. His theme: "I'm going to make you a rich man." He didn't, but he gave me a comfortable retirement. About this time I had dinner with Dan Boorstin, the historian who was then Librarian of Congress. I asked him what he thought of my leaving *The Times* and starting a new publication. "How long have you been at *The Times*," Dan asked. "Only 40 years," I said. Dan replied, "You know, Marty, change is good. You'll be using new muscles, and learning every day." Other friends told me there were two things about a startup: "You'll never work harder, and you'll never have more fun." They were right on both counts.

After Jerry's fourth visit, he suggested I go to New York and talk to some of the publishers of his newspapers.

Tom Allon was the first publisher I saw. He was in his early 30s, a handsome, well-dressed and well-spoken young man. Tom was publisher of two weekly newspapers. His place of business was a loft in the fur district. He had the entire 5th floor of 242 West 30th Street. As it happened, my father's place of business had been the entire 5th floor of 242 West 30th Street, and I knew every inch of the premises. I had picked up fur coats in the spring and delivered them in the fall. I had quickly discovered that the farther out a customer lived, the better my tip. In mid-Manhattan, a maid would usually open the door, take the furs and close the door. But out in Brooklyn or the Bronx, the customer would open the door, take the furs, give me a hot chocolate, some cookies and a handsome tip.

When I got off the elevator, I saw that Tom had his editorial staff on the right, where my father had his showroom. They both had offices in the center, and Tom had his business staff on the left, where my father had his factory. I immediately concluded that I had received a message from the Great Beyond. The message: sign up with Jerry Finkelstein. Later that afternoon, when Jerry invited me to his triplex penthouse on Park Avenue, I told him I had changed my mind. I was ready to work for him. Jerry promptly took out a yellow, legal cap pad, and began writing down numbers: my salary, bonuses, etc. I told him I never negotiated my own contract, and that he should talk to my agent/lawyer, Bob Barnett. At that point I had only met Bob socially. Bob represented celebrity authors, including, most recently, the Obamas and Bill and Hillary Clinton, but when I called him he said he would be happy to represent me. Bob charged by the hour.

This was January 1994. Bob had recently written a contract for the new editor-in-chief of *The Chicago Sun-Times*, which he used as a model for my contract. As both publisher and editor-in-chief, I insisted on a piece of the action. I would not leave *The Times*, where I had worked for 40 years, knew everyone and was extremely comfortable, without an equity interest in whatever I would create. Jerry balked. The negotiations continued until June 30, when he finally relented. Bob charged by the hour, and by that time I had run up a considerable bill. Bob put a clause in the contract that stated that Jerry would pay my legal fees, which he did. *The Times* had announced that it would offer a buyout to senior employees, beginning in September. I went to the publisher, with whom I had done successful labor negotiations, and he told me that I could leave immediately and still receive the buyout. July 1 I was gone. My friends at *The Times* started calling me "Marty the Mogul," having gone from shop steward to publisher in a single day.

It was a big gamble. I was leaving my professional home of 40 years, where I had been treated well and felt reasonably secure. For what? A big question mark. I had never hired anyone or managed anything, except for being *The Times*' convention coordinator at the Democratic and Republican national conventions in 1992. Could I cut the mustard?

The Times was an inestimable help in my transition. Punch Sulzberger, chairman of *The Times* board, gave me an office next to his on West 43rd Street to conduct interviews. He always introduced me as a publisher, and I would always say, "To me I'm a publisher, to my mother I'm a publisher, but to publishers am I a publisher?" Arthur Gelb, my friend who had been *The Times* managing editor, read and critiqued every copy from our beginning until the new year. I would call my editors into my office, put Arthur on the speakerphone and hear his unsparing criticism of each article in every issue. He critiqued everything including story placement, headlines, writing and substance. He gave me a crash course in editing. When Republicans won the House and Senate in November, six weeks after our first issue, Arthur gave me advice that I ignored, to my regret. Speaker Newt Gingrich and the Republicans had campaigned on what they called a "Contract with America," a multi-point agenda that included a balanced budget and lower taxes, and banned family planning. Arthur suggested that our entire front page be devoted to this agenda as a roadmap to Republican legislative intentions. It was a great idea, which I wrongfully reduced to a small box on page one.

Abe Rosenthal, *The Times*' groundbreaking executive editor, also was helpful. He hosted a party in my honor in his Manhattan penthouse, to which he invited the mayor, governor, senators and several moguls who controlled many businesses, with a view to getting them to advertise in *The Hill*. The effort was successful.

I had been a reporter my entire working life, with minimal management experience. In fact the only thing I had managed was being

The Times' convention coordinator during the 1992 Democratic and Republican national conventions. Although the job of *The Times* coordinator had involved many financial transactions, if I ran short of funds I need only call someone at *The Times*, and my account was flush within the hour. Working for Jerry was different. His CEO, Mike Schenkler, was a penny-pincher, who initially didn't even want my reporters to have their own desks or computers. His philosophy: they could share. Mike had strenuously opposed creation of a Washington political newspaper. Every time I needed money, he said "no," and I had to appeal to Jerry, who ultimately said, "yes."

Where to begin? The first thing I needed was office space. I searched the city, with the aid of real estate brokers, and found space at a ridiculously low cost at a building at 15th and H streets NW, in the heart of Washington's former financial district. "Too expensive," said Mike. "Then you find me office space for less," I said. He relented. What next? Someone to design the office. I hired an architect with whom I worked. I wanted my office to have glass walls, so that I could look out at the newsroom, and more importantly, everyone else could look in. Adjoining my office were the offices of the executive editor and the managing editor. Unfortunately, the managing editor was a friend of the architect, whom she persuaded to make her office larger, at the expense of my office. Fortunately, I discovered this before actual construction and made her office even smaller than it had been originally. She didn't last until our first issue, for this and other reasons.

I then needed desks, which I purchased second hand, and a computer network. I knew nothing about computers but found a young man who was knowledgeable, sold me computers and created a server.

Next, I needed someone to design the paper. Should it be a broadsheet, like *The Times*, or a tabloid? How many columns? How large the type? I approached Lou Silverstein, who had designed the modern *New York Times*, including *Science Times* and *Sports Monday*, and *Times*-owned newspapers across the country, including newspapers in Sarasota and Santa Barbara. Lou was a short, balding man who communicated mostly with graphics. He had difficulty speaking, with a very bad stutter. Lou agreed to do it, but his price wasn't just beyond my budget, it was out of this world. I asked Arthur Gelb, who had worked closely with him, to intervene, and his price came down sufficiently to be acceptable.

Next, I needed a staff. The day after I signed my contract with Jerry, *The Times*, *The Washington Post* and *The Wall Street Journal* all published articles about my forthcoming newspaper. I was deluged by friends who had retired from journalism after taking buyouts, as well as children of friends. They all sought editorial jobs, either as editors or reporters. Some of the older ones gave me the impression they were just looking for a warm place to work, and I knew I needed people with lots of energy, and at least two years of journalism experience. Their salaries were low, but we offered great experience and training, and helped them leap to major media organizations whose editors began calling me when they needed someone with Hill experience. When we thought a reporter was ready, we helped him get a job at *The Wall Street Journal*, *The New York Times* and *L.A. Times*, among other publications.

For executive editor, I made the best decision in all my years at *The Hill*. I hired Al Eisele. I had met Al when I covered the Carter administration and he was Vice President Walter F. Mondale's press secretary. He had come to Washington as a correspondent for Knight-Ridder, which owned the newspaper on which he started, the *St. Paul Pioneer Press-Dispatch*. Al had seen the articles in the newspapers heralding a new publication on the Hill, and he called and expressed interest. When I saw him, he had a terrible cold, with red eyes and red nose. He looked ten years older than his age. I scheduled another interview and was sold. Al not only had great news judgment, but was incredibly patient with our reporters, who sat beside him when he edited their copy. I did the same, but without his legendary patience.

Marty Fleming, our first business manager, also proved a very good hire, as was Sheila Casey, who has been *The Hill*'s CFO for many years. Sheila's husband, George, had just been transferred from Denver to Washington. I asked Sheila whom he worked for. "Oh," she said, "he's in the Army." A few weeks later I asked what he did. "Oh," she said, "he's at the Pentagon." A few weeks after that I asked his rank. "He's a general," she said. He came to Washington as a one-star and gained additional stars until he was a four-star who led the U.S. coalition in Iraq and later was appointed Army Chief-of-Staff. Like Al, Sheila had a wonderful way with people, and I'm sure she bore some responsibility for his rise in the military. Al and Sheila had excellent judgment and were my sounding boards before I made any important decisions.

But I knew nothing about advertising sales people. For that I used a head-hunter. We were fortunate to get Fran McMahon as advertising director. She eventually became *The Hill*'s publisher. Finally, I needed a printer and a circulation strategy. The Capitol mailman distributed *Roll Call* to congressional offices without charge, and I persuaded him to do the same for *The Hill*. Several printers submitted proposals, and I took one whose plant was in Rockville, Md.

After several mock trials, our first issue was published Sept. 21, 1994, just seven weeks after I signed my contract. The headline across the top of the front page read, "Foreign PACS Break Record." The subhead read, "On pace in 1994 to exceed spending in last election." The idea came from one of the eight books Sue and I had written, this one on foreign investment in the U.S. Another page one story dealt with the murder of a Senate staffer. Other articles included a story about a congressman with long overdue books loaned from the Library of Congress (some going back four years); a list of key House races, with descriptions of the issues in each race; and an article with a graphic on "Eight key issues facing the 103rd Congress." In addition, I wrote a short-lived gossip column. Our editorial declared our mission to be "Respect the Institution [Congress], but scrutinize its members and policies."

I was 66 years old, working a seven-day week, selling advertising as well as overseeing the business and editorial staffs. I didn't think I could work that hard. I sold our first ad to Bernard Schwartz, chairman of Loral Corporation, who had called after the *Times*, *Wall Street Journal* and *Washington Post* articles. Bernard wanted a subscription. I said we'd comp him, but also wanted an advertising schedule, which he provided. Next, I called Dwayne Andreas, chairman of Archer Daniels Midland, a giant commodities company, whom I had treated none too kindly as a reporter, but he nevertheless also purchased a series of ads. I went down the list of every businessman I knew, and some actually purchased ads.

The bulk of our revenue came from advocacy advertising placed by lobbyists who represented clients that could be affected by legislation before the House or Senate. At one point I received a call from

Ralph Nader, the consumer advocate, who asked, "Well, Marty, how does it feel to publish a billboard for lobbyists?" It was the same sort of trade-off that the mainstream media had pioneered: advertising revenue allowed us to hire reporters and editors and pay all the costs of publishing information essential to the body politic.

We provided a very cost-effective package. Although we only distributed on the Hill, and printed only 24,000 copies, we offered full-page ads for about $5,000, while *The Times* and *The Post* charged hundreds of thousands of dollars. Our targeted audience consisted of the people they wanted to reach: members of the House and Senate, and their staffs. The full-page advertisers in our first issue were Merrill Lynch (back page), Phillip Morris, National Journal, Lexis-Nexis (two-page spread), the Manocherian Foundation (an automobile safety organization) and the Senate Federal Credit Union, in addition to Loral and ADM.

The Hill published every Wednesday when Congress was in session. Like Congress, we took most of August off. Eventually, *The Hill* published daily. We also had an extremely active web site that rivaled the major media in the number of hits we received. Some accused us of changing the nature of journalism. When I was a reporter and covered a morning event such as a news conference, I had many hours to do research and interviews before filing my stories. Today, when there is a morning event, reporters file web articles hourly. Has this hurt the dissemination of news? You decide.

One bright spot midway through my time at *The Hill*: I did a two-year stint as a Pulitzer juror. My best friend William Safire had arranged the honor. The juries met in conference rooms at Columbia University's famed School of Journalism, where I had been an Associate in Journalism when I was City Hall bureau chief. This meant being followed by a journalism student, whom I tutored for a period of time as I performed my journalistic tasks. There were five reporters and/or editors on about a dozen Pulitzer juries. Judging took almost a week. The first year my subject was explanatory journalism, everything from science and math to the arts. We were the last jury to recommend three nominees, the winner to be selected by the board. My second year I was on the commentary jury, judging opinion columns on absolutely everything. We also labored long into the last night.

When I began *The Hill*, our rival, *Roll Call*, thought that advertising with us was sheer folly. Their editor, asked to comment on the new publication, confidently predicted that we wouldn't be around more than six months. Asked to reply, I always lauded *Roll Call* as a very good newspaper that should be must reading for anyone who worked on the Hill. But I added that we also were must reading, and so we became. *The Hill* recently celebrated its 24th birthday.

After a few months my friend Pat Choate made me an offer I couldn't refuse. He was working with the United Auto Workers to create a national network of several hundred small local radio stations. He wanted to broadcast an hour-long call-in show every morning from our office, on national politics. One of the advantages was that we had members of Congress in our offices for interviews almost every morning. Our first guest was Speaker Newt Gingrich. The Republicans, who had won the congressional elections in 1994, had been largely ignored by *Roll Call*, and appreciated the arrival of another publication on the Hill.

Jerry had another idea: a day-long forum in January, when Congress was out of session, featuring key legislators discussing the issues their committees would be dealing with. (As if I didn't have enough to do.) I rented the ballroom of the Hyatt Hotel on Capitol Hill, and invited the Republican chairman and Democratic ranking members of every major Senate committee to speak for 15 minutes and take 15 minutes of questioning. Every chairman and ranking member accepted my invitation. We invited the public and even served lunch. Our luncheon speaker was, who else? Bill Safire. As a result, TV cameras from every network showed up, because little else was happening on the Hill. Only one senator didn't show up: Daniel Patrick Moynihan, a Democrat from my home state, New York. I had known Pat for many years, and we had had a cordial relationship. Until we ran a story that he didn't like. Pat was miffed by an article about how one of his top staffers went home to New York every evening and returned the following morning, at taxpayer expense. In any event, Senator John McCain preceded Moynihan's scheduled appearance and graciously agreed to extend his remarks to occupy the void created by Moynihan's absence. The forum gave us a full issue of cutting edge articles.

Although *The Hill* had broken several stories our first year, we really came into our own the second year with an article by Sandy Hume, the son of Britt Hume, the Fox newscaster. Britt had called me to get a job for Sandy, who was quickly promoted from news assistant to reporter. He had excellent sources among Republicans. The story he broke dealt with an attempted Republican coup against Speaker Newt Gingrich. The article went around the world, and I decorated our entrance hall with the front pages of the story cited in newspapers in London, Paris, Rome and other cities.

Sandy also gave me my worst moments at *The Hill*. He had had a childhood issue with alcohol. Sandy had been on the wagon for several years but went to a basketball game one night and drank several beers. He then drove his companion home, after which he was stopped by a police officer for drunken driving. He gave the policeman lip and was placed in the D.C. jail, where he tried to hang himself. A psychiatrist who examined him the following morning pronounced him good to go. Sandy went home, put a rifle in his mouth and ended his life. He was 28.

After the funeral, I took the staff to the Cosmos Club for lunch. We all talked about Sandy, who had always appeared happy-go-lucky. He would often come into my office with a joke. None of us could have predicted such an ending. I hired a psychologist to hold sessions with our staff, which was paralyzed with grief. I then created a Sandy Hume Memorial Award for the best political reporting by someone under 35. I had to come up with $25,000 for the National Press Club to administer the $1,000 annual award, which they did. Nearly everyone on the paper contributed, as did Sandy's many friends. Cleaning out Sandy's desk and, accompanied by Sue, giving the contents to his mother was the worst single day of my life at *The Hill*.

Our reporters developed excellent sources. We were resolutely nonpartisan. The Republicans, out of power for many years, were thrilled to have a publication that was interested in them. And the Democrats were pleased that although out of power, there was a publication that sought them out. We hired reporters who had at least two years' experience on other publications and gave them an education in journalism.

After nine years, Jerry decided we should go daily. I was still working hard just to produce a weekly, but not nearly as hard as I had worked that first year. I thought running a daily, at the age of 75, would be a bit too much. I decided to retire and write another book with Susan. I sold my equity interest. Jerry had not made me rich, but he had made me comfortable. Dan Boorstin had been right. I had used brain cells I had never used before. Change *was* good.

Two years later I received a call from Bob Barnett, my lawyer. Robert Albritton had tried to buy *The Hill*, but the price, $45 million, was too high. Robert now wanted to start his own paper. Would I be interested in helping him? I was then 76 years old. *The Hill* had failed to require a no-compete clause in my contract, and I was free to accept. I told him I would, if the price was right, but only for three years, to hire a staff and help them get launched. It was different than starting *The Hill*. The Albritton headquarters was in Roslyn, just across the Potomac River from Washington, not 200 miles away in New York. There was no penny pinching. They did not want neophytes whom we would train, whom we hired at *The Hill*, but experienced reporters with name recognition. When I submitted my first budget, Robert and his CEO Fred Ryan told me "Not enough. Add a million dollars," words that never crossed the lips of either the Sulzbergers or Finkelsteins, for whom I had worked. Fred is now publisher of *The Washington Post*. Nor did I have to look for office space. Robert owned a network of TV stations on the Atlantic Coast, including two stations in Washington. We would share their space.

As with *The Hill*, I was inundated by applicants for editorial jobs after the announcement that I was starting a new publication. Many of the applicants were journalistic friends who had taken buyouts from mainstream publications that were reducing their staffs. Many of them had had distinguished careers. But many of those applicants looked tired, even defeated. It was hard to reject them, but I knew that a startup needed people with lots of energy and optimism.

How to differentiate *Politico* from *The Hill* and *Roll Call*, which had been publishing 40 years when *The Hill* began, but failed to improve its product in light of the new competition. Although *The Hill* was hard hitting and broke scores of stories, it also had more articles on the culture of Congress, including book, movie and restaurant reviews. At one point *The Hill* had two gossip columns. As its name suggested, *Politico* focused almost exclusively on politics. Unlike *Politico*, *The Hill* also had an editorial page. Because I could pay higher salaries at

Politico, I hired more experienced reporters and editors than I could at *The Hill*. We lured them from major publications including *The Washington Post* and *Time* magazine. To persuade reporters and editors to take the risk of leaving comfortable jobs at those publications to work for a startup that may or may not succeed, our salaries were among the best in the business. *Roll Call* meanwhile continued to publish as if *The Hill* and *Politico* did not exist, and became almost irrelevant.

Doyle McManus, editor of the *Los Angeles Times* Washington bureau, said that I had raised journalistic salaries all over Washington, as mainstream news organizations had to increase their salaries to retain reporters and editors I was wooing. As a former shop steward, this made me feel great. *Politico* also had two people whose sole job was to get reporters on national television news shows. They did a great job and easily caught up to the national exposure received by *The Hill's* reporters.

By flooding the Capitol with scores of reporters, *The Hill* and *Politico* changed the culture of Congress. This meant much greater coverage than the legislators had previously received. Reporters from *The Hill* and *Politico* poked their noses everywhere. It became much harder for legislators to conceal their actions and ambitions. *The Hill* and *Politico* also changed the media. Because those publications produced online articles 24/7, the mainstream media also had to do so. When events occurred in the morning, there was no waiting until evening to produce an article. Instead, reporters had to file every hour or so. The mainstream media became much more aggressive and garnered Pulitzer Prizes for its coverage of President Trump. There was talk that *The Hill* and *Politico* had become sweatshops, overworking their staffs, which were deprived of time to relax and think. In its early days, there was considerable turnover at *Politico*. To compete with the two publications, mainstream publications also had to increase their coverage of Congress. *The Times* and *The Washington Post*, which previously had two people reporting on Congress, added several more.

My title was senior publisher and editor. I hired about 80 people, both editorial and business. One of them, Matt Wuerker, our cartoonist, won a Pulitzer Prize a few years later. I got Lou Silverstein, who had designed *The Hill*, to design their newspaper, and found them a printer, circulation director and took care of all their needs. I had settled on a title, "The Capitol Leader." I had a hard time finding an editor, and wooed Jim Vanden Hei, *The Washington Post*'s star political reporter, with three lunches at the University Club. He eventually became executive editor and brought in his friend John Harris, *The Post*'s political editor, as editor-in-chief. Jim's wife, Autumn, came up with the name *Politico*. When I encountered Ben Bradlee, *The Post*'s famed editor, at social occasions, he indicated he was not pleased by my thievery. *Politico* launched in January 2007. Both *Politico* and *The Hill* have become highly successful money machines. I was proud of my role in creating both publications.

With so many mainstream publications cutting back or closing, it's extraordinary that these two publications have been thriving. *Politico* now has 200 employees, mostly reporters and editors, with publications in New York, Chicago, L.A. and a European edition based in Brussels. *The Hill* has more than 100 employees.

How to account for their success? Both are niche publications, delivering political news to a relatively small number of people. Their print editions go only to members of Congress, congressional staffs, and a few universities and foreign embassies. They both make their money from advocacy advertising, lobbyists, unions and others who want to send a message to Congress.

The Hill and *Politico* were criticized by both politicians and journalists for ushering in 24/7 coverage of the political scene. Traditionally, journalists working for morning publications had all day to interview, research, think and reflect on their work before submitting their articles, and politicians had all day to shape their responses. With the advent of the internet, *The Hill* and *Politico* accelerated the process, making it look more like the speeded-up projections of old silent movies. Reporters covering a morning event, such as a congressional hearing, now have to file every hour on their web sites, without the benefit of interviews, research, thinking or reflection. To compete with *The Hill* and *Politico*, the major news organizations were forced to expand their political staffs and follow suit in speeding up the process of delivering the news. These changes were probably inevitable since the creation of the internet, but *The Hill* and *Politico* pointed the way. Both publications are highly profitable because they reach a targeted audience—politicians and their staffs—at a minimal cost to advertisers. A full page in these publications costs 20% as much as those advertisements in the major media.

We also have forced the mainstream media to devote many more reporters and editors to congressional and political coverage. This is all to the good. Many significant decisions are made behind the scenes, and we forced the mainstream media to dig deeper in their political and congressional coverage.

7

LIFE AFTER JOURNALISM

In my retirement, Sue and I wrote our seventh book: *A World Ignited: How Apostles of Ethnic, Religious and Racial Hatred Torch the Globe.* Our books have taken about three years, from inception to publication. But I'm a hopeless extrovert and need people to bounce ideas off, both in work and play. Ultimately, I found the perfect place.

The Woodrow Wilson International Center for Scholars is a government think tank, populated mostly by academics from all over the world. It is housed in the Reagan building, the second largest office building in Washington, after the Pentagon. Its neighbors include the Environmental Protection Agency and the Secret Service. I wrote to the Wilson Center's director, former Representative Lee Hamilton, a tall, high school and college basketball star who became chairman of the House Foreign Affairs Committee. After a year's wait, I was accepted. It was a six-month term that stretched to six years. I was paid only for the first six months. At first I had a large office overlooking a plaza. In ensuing years, my office space shrunk, eventually to a carrel.

The Wilson Center is the best place in the world to write a book. The Center has a good relationship with the Library of Congress, and a wonderful librarian. During our first week, all the newcomers were marched to the Library of Congress and given staffers to help us. I was given considerable help by both a historian and a political scientist in our quest to find out the effect, if any, of the Supreme Court decision that banned patronage. I did my writing at the Wilson Center. The book became *Pinstripe Patronage: Political Favoritism From the Clubhouse to the White House and Beyond*. We discovered that the Supreme Court decision had little impact in the real world, where patronage continued to flourish.

The Center had many strategies to encourage collegiality. Its government-subsidized cafeteria has only large round tables seating ten, so that one was always surrounded by other "scholars," many from foreign lands working on subjects one knew absolutely nothing about. Lee Hamilton made a point of eating in the cafeteria almost every day, and flitting from table to table. At the end of a six-month term, he knew almost everybody's name and project. Another strategy was periodic status reports to the group on what you had discovered, and where you were going. Finally, you had to conduct a symposium on your completed work. At my symposium I declared that patronage was one of the occupational hazards of a democracy. A dozen hands shot up, and I learned that patronage, giving special benefits to loyalists, was world-wide, especially in fascist and communist countries where elites were given special health facilities, markets, dachas, and other privileges and luxuries. Lee was very kind to me and arranged a public symposium when my work was completed. When Lee retired he was replaced by Jane Harman, a former congresswoman whose specialty was foreign affairs. I'd known Jane since she worked in the Carter White House, when we occasionally had lunch together. Her beautiful face now appears on numerous TV interviews, panels, international conferences and public broadcasting shows.

Life Lessons

Five Things I Learned in More Than 60 Years as a Journalist

1. Courage is crucial. Accomplishing anything means going against the grain, ruffling feathers, upsetting the status quo. This was true for Galileo, Martin Luther, Eugene O'Neil and Franklin D. Roosevelt. It's true for everyone, especially journalists. And it's

true for you. My favorite prayer, a prayer for healing, contains the following passage:

> May the source of strength
> Who blessed the ones before me
> Help me find the courage
> To make my life a blessing.

First, God is not going to bestow courage, but help one find it. Second, the objective is not talent or money or good fortune, but courage, the underpinning of everything worth having in life. Third, you're not asking for fame or fortune, but to make your life a blessing. How does one do that?

2. Live life to the fullest. In the words of the direct mail advertising man who set me on the path toward journalism: Follow Your Dream. Initiate, don't respond. Decide your own career path and ignore the naysayers.

3. Work like hell. In his first speech after Tony Williams became Mayor of Washington, D.C., he told city employees, "I never want to hear a city employee tell someone "I don't know." If one doesn't know the answer to a question, a far better response is: "I'll find out." Friends told me two things about a start-up: You'll never work harder, and you'll never have more fun. When I started *The Hill*, at age 66, and *Politico*, when I was 79, I didn't think I could work that hard. Or have so much fun.

4. Value integrity, kindness, generosity, love. They will be returned manifold, in ways impossible to imagine.

5. Don't neglect your family. They are your foundation. Unlike most others, they will be there your entire life. They will be the ultimate measure of your success in life.

From time to time I speak at colleges and universities, most recently the University of Utah's Hinckley Institute of Politics. There and everywhere else, I was asked if I would recommend a career in journalism, with all the turmoil that now exists. I tell the students that there is no more exciting career. If you're interested in people and ideas, enjoy constantly learning and want to have an impact on your community, nation and world, you should seriously consider a career in journalism. It's given me a great ride.

8

A NEW DAY IN JOURNALISM

I had naturally assumed that when I retired from *The Times*, the quality of the newspaper would plummet. Instead, it has soared. So have *The Washington Post, The Wall Street Journal, Los Angeles Times* and many other mainstream newspapers. They have been helped by the competition from *The Hill, Politico*, as well as blogs, tweets and other forms of online communication.

As noted, the internet has given everyone with a computer access to the public prints, not just zillionaires who could afford the huge costs of printing presses and huge staffs. Cell phones have given nearly everyone the ability to be news photographers, and place photographs on the web.

On Oct. 29, 2011, the leading stories on NBC news were all illustrated by videos taken by bystanders. They involved "Occupy Wall Street" demonstrations in three cities. In Washington, D.C. police officers threw a disabled man out of his wheelchair. He had been verbally taunting the police. In Oakland, California, a tear gas canister fractured the skull of a Vietnam veteran, while in New York City a police inspector fired tear gas on peaceful demonstrators. All the videos went viral. The Oakland video was taken by a woman who was standing on her lawn and was subsequently arrested and released. Thanks to cell phones, any police officer who shoots, beats or otherwise abuses an unarmed person can expect to be on the evening news.

The Times hired reporters from *The Hill* and *Politico*, including David Grann, who went on to write two best-sellers made into movies; Jennifer Senior, a book critic and opinion writer; Kenneth Vogel, a crackerjack investigative reporter, and Jonathan Martin, an ace political reporter. Thus, *The Hill* and *Politico* both have played a role in enhancing *The Times*, among other mainstream publications.

But nothing has done more to enhance journalism than the presidency of Donald Trump. There's nothing like a strong adversary to whet the appetites of journalists, and President Trump has accused the journalistic community of being an "enemy of the people" and publishing "fake news." Marty Baron, the superb editor of *The Washington Post*, had to remind his staff that although President Trump was at war with *The Post*, the newspaper was not at war with the president, merely doings its job collecting and reporting the news. Both *The Times* and *The Post* won Pulitzer Prizes in 2018.

Nevertheless, there are legitimate concerns about the internet's impact on the mainstream media, which has lost most of its advertising revenue in this century. Advertising revenue dropped from $63.5 billion to $23 billion from 2000 to 2013, according to the Brookings Institution. Classified advertising has declined from 40 percent of newspaper advertising revenue to 18 percent. *(Jeremy Litton, Five Myths about Journalism, The Washington Post, Feb. 24, 2019, p. B2).* During that period, a third of all newsroom jobs vanished. More than $2 billion spent on newsgathering disappeared. With less to offer readers, newspaper readership also eroded. The weakened newspapers attracted predatory publishers. Some newspapers and chains were picked up by large conglomerates and hedge funds only interested in bleeding money out of them.

Although the public is still leery of what it reads in the press, public trust in the press is increasing. A Gallup Poll published in the fall of 2018 found that 45 percent of Americans trust the press a great deal or a fair amount, up from an all-time low of 32 percent in 2016, but still off its all-time peak of 72 percent in 1976. This statistic has a partisan divide. A total of 76 percent of Democrats said they trusted the press, but only 42 percent of independents and 21 percent of Republicans. (ibid).

Technological advances in communications occurred before the internet—radio and television being the latest examples—and have largely benefited society. "Each new method of communication made the exchange of information easier, more textured, and more meaningful. Each advance in form and efficiency also had a democratizing influence: As more people became more knowledgeable, they also became better able to question their world and the behavior of people and institutions that directed their lives" (Bill Kovach and Tom Rosensteil, *Blur: How to Know What's Trued in the Age of Information Overload*, New York, Bloomsbury, 2010, p. 12).

Has the quality of the mainstream media been a victim of the internet? Sig Gissler, former administrator of the Pulitzer Prize, noted the decline in the number of entries in the decade after he was appointed. "The volume is down, but the final choices are very strong," he said. "The watchdog still barks." (Interview)

Investigative journalism has been augmented by the internet and niche publications like *The Hill* and *Politico*, as well as new organizations including *ProPublica*, which supply funds and personnel for investigative reporting. The Monica Lewinsky scandal, which led to the impeachment of President Clinton, was first reported by a blogger, Matt Drudge. *The Hill* newspaper, published online and in print, reported an attempted coup against then Speaker Newt Gingrich. The internet played a key role in the investigation of the Penn State sex abuse scandal. "A critical break in the investigation of Jerry Sandusky came via a posting on the internet: a random mention that a Penn State football coach, years before, might have seen something ugly but kept silent" (Jo Becker, *"Inquiry Grows Into Concerns of a Cover-Up,"* New York Times, Nov. 17, 2011, p. B11).

More recently, *The Hill* reported a revolt among Republican senators, including Republican leader Mitch McConnell, against President Trump's government shutdown in early 2019, reporting that they excoriated Vice President Mike Pence at a closed door meeting (Alexander Bolton, *GOP Senators Read Pence Riot Act Before Shutdown Votes*, Jan. 24, 2019). Meanwhile, *Politico* published scoops that led to the resignations of Interior Secretary Ryan Zinke, who stood to benefit financially from his decision to open public lands to oil exploration (story published June 19, 2018, resigned December 21, 2018); Health and Human Services Secretary Tom Price, who with his wife took military jets to Europe and Asia at a cost of $500,000 (story published September 28, 2017, and resigned next day); Brenda Fitzgerald, Director of the Centers for Disease Control, who purchased tobacco stock (story published Jan. 30, 2018, resigned next day), and Labor Secretary nominee Andrew Puzders, who was accused of spousal abuse (reported Feb. 15, 2017, withdrew his nomination same day).

Critics of the new media decry the loss of professionalism, the fact-checking and experience that were the hallmark of the best of the mainstream media, as well as its role as "gatekeeper," deciding what the public should know. No fact-checkers exist to second-guess what could be serious errors floating about in the blogosphere, although the blogosphere is somewhat self-correcting—a torrent of comments quickly point out factual errors. But the mainstream media has a checkered record—including articles about Iraq's weapons of mass destruction, which proved non-existent but nevertheless led to the Iraq war. And, as previously noted, "gatekeeping" was sometimes used to benefit publishers, as in their worshipful reporting on Robert Moses.

Indeed, every phase of journalism's evolution has had its downside. The printing press provided wide distribution of both the Bible and *Mein Kampf.* Early radio gave us both the inspiring voice of Franklin D. Roosevelt and the anti-Semitic demagogue Father Coughlin. Fast, cheap and efficient, the internet has helped organize both liberation movements and terrorist activities.

Lest we forget, the mainstream media also had its spurious side. Yellow journalism and sensationalism ("Headless Woman in Topless Bar," a famous *N.Y. Post* headline) were the stock in trade, not just of tabloids, but also some more respected publications. Some of those publications became captives of the government, special interests, and worse.

One of the major challenges of internet readers is to sift through the thousands of blogs and determine which are relevant and credible. Among the blogs that do their own reporting are *The Daily Beast* and *Huffington Post.* In effect, readers must be their own editors. But this was always the case. Nevertheless, it's sometimes difficult to discern the viewpoint of a blogger. Is he biased? Comprehensive? Analytical? What is her world view? Does she share your basic view of the world?

Will readers be able to discern quality from fakery, news from rumor and hoaxes?

The stakes are enormously high, with democracy itself hanging in the balance. Indeed, the media has played a major role in the nation's social progress, from television news bringing the abuses against civil rights protesters in the south into America's living rooms, to *The Washington Post*'s role in exposing Watergate, and from *The New York Fs* demonstrating the futility of the Vietnam War to videographers showing the murder of unarmed black men.

The march of history suggests that society is up to the challenge.

INDEX

Note: Page numbers in *italics* indicate figures.

100–Year Association 34

Abzug, Bella 52
advertisers 92–93
Agger, Carolyn 53
Agnew, Spiro 48
Albert, Carl 67
Albritton Robert 96
Aldrin, Buzz 19
Allon, Tom 88
American Psychiatric Association 36
amphetamines 48
Andreas, Dwayne 92
anxiety attacks 36–37
Archer Daniels Midland 92
Argentine Diary (Josephs) 5
Armstrong, Neil 18
Army: basic training 14–15;
    discharge 4, 8–9, 16–17
Arnold, Marty 33
August (Rossner) 32

Baker, Howard H. Jr. 71–72
Baker, James A. 67
Baker, James III 72
Baquet, Dean 27
Barclay, Dorothy 21, *22*, 24
Barnett, Bob 88, 96
Baron, Marty 106

baseball game, Shea Stadium 44
Bazelon, David 83–84
Beame, Abe 41
Beard, Robin 77
Begin, Menachem 73–74
Benchley, Peter 31
Bender, Marylin 22
Berger, Meyer 17, 26
Biaggi, Mario 51, 58–59
Bible 2, 108
Bigart, Homer 17, 22
Binn, Sheldon 26
Blackout Babies, New York City
    maternity wards 37
blacks: bigotry against 65;
    journalists 27
blogs 108
Blumenstein, Rebecca 27
Blur (Kovach and Rosensteil) 107
Book Find Club 4
Boorstin, Dan 87, 96
Boston Globe, The (newspaper) 71
Bradlee, Ben 98
Bradley, Richard (Pete) 12
British Vogue (magazine) 23
Brody, Jane 24
Bronx Science 9–10, 12
Brookings Institution 106
Brother, The (Roberts) 7–8

Brzezinski, Zbigniew 72, 74
Buckley, James 54
Buckley, William 54
Bumiller, Elisabeth 27
Burnham, David 7, 30, 63
Burritt, Richard 21
Buying Into America (Tolchin &
    Tolchin) 77
Buzz Aldrin Day 18
Byrd, Robert 66–67

Carey, Hugh 58, 59–60
Carlson, John Roy 4
Carnegie Hall 15
Caro, Robert 3, 30
Carter, Jimmy 9, 72, *73*, 74, 102
Casey, Sheila 91
Catledge, Turner, 36
cauls 59
Chicago Sun-Times, The (newspaper)
    88
Children Who Hate (Redl) 21
Choate, Pat 94
Chronicle, The (newspaper) 13
Civil Rights 64
Claiborne, Craig 22
Clifford, Clark 8
Clinton, Bill 88, 107
Clinton, Hillary 65, 88
Collins, Al (Jazzbo) 13
Columbia Law School 14
Columbia University 93
Committee on Character and
    Fitness 6, 16
communications, technological
    advances 107
communists 7, 65, 81, 102
Congress, five myths about 64–66
Contract with America 89
copy boys 1, 6, 17–20
corruption: campaign against,
    29–30; New York City police
    department 7
Corso, Dominic L. 43
Coughlin, Father 108
Counsel to the President (Clifford) 8
Crowell, Paul 37

Cunningham, Ed (Rev.) 12
Cuomo, Mario 43
Curtis, Charlotte 22
Cystic Fibrosis 47

Daily Beast, The (blog) 108
D'Amato, Al 67
dances 32–33
Daniel, Clifton 54
Deaver, Michael 81–82
democratization of journalism 2
Dent, Harry 53
dentist, anesthetic deaths and 37
DeSapio, Carmine 35
Dewey, Thomas E. 13
Diamond, Stuart 81
Dingell, John 82
Dixie Hotel 27
Donovan, Carrie 22
Drudge, Matt 107
Durk, David 29, 30

Eagleton Tom 48
Eastland James 57, 65
Einstein, Albert 65
Eisele, Al 91
Eizenstat, Stuart 74
Emerson, Gloria 22
English, Arnold 18
Epstein, Jason 45
Ervin, Sam 57
Everett M. Dirksen Award for
    Distinguished Reporting of
    Congress 72

fact-checkers 108
Fake News 3, 4, 106
Falk, Lee 31–32
Feinstein, Dianne 66
Felker, Clay 46
Ferretti, Fred 44
Finkelstein, Jerry 87, 88, 90, 95–96
Fitzgerald, Brenda 108
Fleming, Marty 91
Ford, Gerald 59
Foreign Policy Association 34–35
Fortas, Abe 53

Fox, Sylvan 30
Frankel, Max 52, 82
Frasco, Frank 52
Ft. Benjamin Harrison 15
Ft. Bliss, Texas 14
Furbows 13

Galileo 102
Gallup Poll 106
Garcia, Robert 52
gatekeeping/gatekeeper 3, 108
Gelb, Arthur 9, 24–25, 30, 44, 49,
    82, 89, 90; photograph *26*; prank
    on 44
German, Geoffrey 3
Gheraldi, Angelo 19
Gingrich, Newt 71, 89, 94, 107
Girls in the Balcony, The (Robertson) 23
Gissler, Sig 107
"Golden Fleece" awards 60
Goldsmith, Susan 29, 31, 34; *see also*
    Tolchin, Martin and Sue
Goldstein, David 23
"good old days" of politics 57
Grann, David 106
Greenglass, David 7
Griscom, Tom 72

Hagerty, Gil 44
Halberstam, David 7
Hamilton, Lee 102
Hamilton, Thomas Jefferson, Jr. 20
Harman, Jane 102
Harris, John 98
Hearst, William Randolph 3
Hecht, Ben 54
Helms, Jesse 57, 65
Hepburn, Katherine 5
Herbers, John 81
Hersh, Seymour 63
Hershman, Morris 19
Hill, The (newspaper) 2, 5, 98,
    103, 105; advertisers of 89,
    92–93; advertising salesman
    at 78; Albritton and 96;
    anniversary 94; daily publication
    93; differentiating *Politico* from

96–98; founding of 4, 6;
    investigative journalism 107; rival
    Roll Call and 94, 96–97; Sandy
    Hume at 95; staff of 91–92, 96
Hills, Carla 70–71
Hills, Roderick 61
Hinkley Institute of Politics 103
Hiss, Alger 8
holocaust survivors 19
hospitals: Blackout Babies at 37;
    protests at 36; reporting on
    New York 33–34, 35
Howkins, Elizabeth Penrose 23
"How to Get a Job" course 16–17
Huffington Michael 66
Huffington Post (blog) 108
Hume, Britt 95
Hume, Sandy 95
Humphrey, Hubert 75
Huxtable, Ada Louise 83

Idaho State Bengal (newspaper) 12
Idaho State College 10, 11–12
Inner Circle annual dinner 39
insider trading 41–42
International Labor Organization 77
internet 2, 3, 98, 105–108
invasion of privacy 54
Iran Contra investigation 75
Iraqi POWS 63

Jacobson, Max (aka Dr. Feelgood) 48
Javits, Jacob 52, 59
Jaws (Benchley) 31
Jews 57, 59; denigrating 57; Lindsay's
    problems with 42–43, 48; raising
    children 24; respect for 12
Johns Hopkins 47
Johnson, Frank 83
Johnson, Lyndon 7
Jones, Dave 63
Jordan, Hamilton 74
Josephs, Ray 5
journalism: democratization of 2;
    evolution of 2–3; investigative
    107; yellow 108
journalist, definition 2

Kassebaum, Nancy 72
Kempton Murray 38
Kennedy, Jackie 48
Kennedy, John F. 48, 68, 74
Kennedy, Ted 55, 56
Kerouac, Jack 26
Kirkland, Lane 78
Kissinger, Henry 52, 56
Koch, Ed 56, 58
Korean War 14, 17, 30
Kriegel, Jay 29
Ku Klux Klan 66
Kurzman, Steve 52
Kylshiski, Lucas 47

Landauer, Jerry 19
Landon, Alf 72
Lazard Frere 60, 61
Lerner, Alan Jay 49
Lewinsky, Monica 107
Lewis, Neil 81
Lexis-Nexis 93
Liberty Mutual Liability Insurance
    Company 16
Librium 36
Life (magazine) 31
life lessons 102–103
Lindsay, John Vliet 34, 38, 49;
    campaign for presidency 48;
    conflict with reporters 39–40;
    mayor of New York City 38–42;
    photograph *40*; problems with
    Jews 42–43, 48
Linowitz, Sol 78
Long, Russell 57
Look (magazine) 42
Loral Corporation 92
Los Angeles Times (newspaper) 97
Loyalty Oath, Truman 8
Luce, Bill 26
Luther, Martin 102

Macy's 41
Manocherian Foundation 93
Man of the House (O'Neill) 71
Manson, Peter (Lt. Col.) 15–16
Marcantonio, Vito 10

Martin, Jonathan 106
Matthews, Chris 71
Mazzia, Tino 33–34
McCain, John 66, 94
McCarthyism 7, 8
McClellan, John 57, 65
McConnell, Mitch 107
McCormack, John 58
McMahon, Fran 92
McMahon, Linda 66
McManus, Doyle 97
McNamara, Robert 7
Medicaid and Medicare 33
Mein Kampf 2, 108
Merrill Lynch 93
Metzenbaum, Howard 80
Michel, Bob 71
Miller, Arthur 31
Miller, William "Fishbait" 52
Minneapolis Tribune, The
    (newspaper) 24
Mohr, Charlie 63, 72
Molotsky, Irv 54
Mondale, Walter 75, 91
Morath, Inge 31
Morgan, Tom 42
Moses, Robert 3, 29, 30, 108
Moynihan, Daniel Patrick 52, 94
Murphy, John 52
Museum of Modern Art 18

Nader, Ralph 93
National Institutes of Health 21, 47
National Journal 93
National Press Club 23, 95
Naughton, Jim 63
Nazi concentration camps 19
Newspaper Guild 1, 5
New York (magazine) 45–46
New York Bight 31
New York City, financial crisis
    59–61
New York Daily News (newspaper)
    17, 26, 59
New Yorker, The (magazine) 45
New York Herald Tribune
    (newspaper) 53

New York Law School 14
New York Post, The (newspaper) 17, 32
New York's Garment Center 5
New York Times, The (newspaper)
    1–2, 4, 71, 72, 74, 90, 91, 109;
    convention coordinator 10; copy
    boy's at 6, 17, 27; design of 90;
    Gelb at 9, 24–25, *26*, 30, 44, 49,
    82, 89, 90; hazing newcomers at
    27–28; romances at 27; Rosenthal
    at 9, 22–25, *25*, 30, 41, 42, 49,
    53, 54, 89; strike by printers 5;
    Trump and 3–4, 84; Washington
    bureau 63, 77–80
New York University 14
Nicaraguan contras 75
Night Rewrite 28–29
Nixon, Richard 52, 54
North, Oliver 76
NYTimes Foundation 82

Obama, Barack 66, 88
O'Brien, George 22
"Occupy Wall Street"
    demonstrations 105
O'Neill, Eugene 25, 102
O'Neill, Thomas P. Jr. (Tip) 56, 58,
    65, 67–71, *69*, 81

Pacino, Al 30
Parrott, Lindsay 20
Paul the Miser 18
Pear, Robert 63
Pence, Mike 107
Phillip Morris 93
picket lines 5–6
Pinstripe Patronage (Tolchin &
    Tolchin) 102
Podell, Bert 52
Politico (publication) 2, 5, 7, 103,
    105; differentiating *The Hill*
    from 96–98; employees 98, 106;
    founding of 4, 6; investigative
    journalism 107; name 98
Powell, Jody 74
Power Broker, The (Caro) 3, 30
Price, Tom 107

Primus, Lance 78–79
printing press 2
Procaccino, Mario 41
professionalism 108
ProPublica 107
Proxmire, William 60
public dances 32–33
Pulitzer Prize 97; cartoonist Matt
    Wuerker 97; entries for 107;
    Homer Bigart 22; Meyer Berger,
    26; Nan Robertson 22; *The Times*
    and *The Post* 106; *Washington Post*
    for Nixon investigation 52
Puzders, Andrew 108

Rankin, John 65
Rayburn, Sam 68–70
Reagan, Ronald 67, 68, 75, 81
Redl, Fritz 21
Reid, Ogden, Jr. 53
reporters as "enemies of the
    people" 3
reporting as balancing act 22
Reston James "Scotty" 52, 53
R.H. Macy & Co. 41
Ribicoff, Abraham 59
Richmond, Fred 52
Roberts, Gene 48, 63
Roberts, Sam 7
Robertson, Nan 22
Rockefeller, Mary 42
Rockefeller, Nelson 42, 56
Rockefeller Foundation 79
Rohatyn, Felix 60, 61
Roll Call (newspaper) 87, 92, 94,
    96–97
Rooney, John 58
Roosevelt, Franklin D. 34, 102, 108
Rosenberg, Ethel 7
Rosenberg, Julius 7
Rosenthal, Abe 9, 22–25, 30, 41,
    42, 49, 53, 54, 89; dispute with
    32–33; photo of *25*
Rosenthal, Ben 51, 52
Rossner, Judith 32
Russell, Richard 57, 64
Ryan, Fred 96

Sadat, Anwar 73–74
Safire, William 9, 10, 53, 54–55, 73, 93, 94
St. Paul Pioneer Press-Dispatch (newspaper) 91
Sales, Cornelius Calvin, Jr. 66; *see also* Byrd, Robert
Salisbury, Harrison 17, 32
Sandusky, Jerry 107
Sandy Hume Memorial Award 95
Sasser, James 77
Scalia, Antonin 46
Schaefer, Rudy *40*
Schecter, Jerry 73
Scherman, David 31
Scheuer, Jim 58
Schlenker, Mike 90
Schlossberg, Nancy 77
Schlossberg, Steve 77, 78
School of Journalism 93
Schwartz, Bernard 92
Science Times (newspaper) 90
Securities and Exchange Commission 61
Seeger, Pete 5
Seeker's Club, The 12
Senate Federal Credit Union 93
Senior, Jennifer 106
sensationalism 108
Serpico, Frank 29, 30
Shabecoff, Phil 63
Shakow, Patricia 52
Shea Stadium 44, 83
Sheehan, Neil 7
Sher, Roger 29
Sherrill, Bob 48
Shumach, Murray 17
Silverstein, Lou 90, 97
Simon, William 60
Simpson, Alan 81
Simpson–Mazzoli immigration bill of 1986 81
Smith, Hedrick 66
Smith, Howard 65
Smith, Red 72
Smith, Terry 72, *73*
South Bronx 49
South Korea 81
Sparkman, John 57

Spiegel, Irving 26
Sports Monday (newspaper) 90
Steingut, Stanley 44–45
Stennis, John 57
strikes 5–6, 43
Students for Wallace 13
Sulzberger, A. G. 4
Sulzberger, Arthur Ochs, Jr. 78, *79*
Sulzberger, Arthur Ochs "Punch" Sr. 7, 89
Sunday Magazine 23; "Parent & Child" column 24
Sunday Review (New York Times) 82
Swetnick, George 44
Syms, Steve 82

Talese, Gay 83
Talmadge, Eugene 65
Tames, George 71
Taylor, Glenn 13
Teltsch, Kathleen 20
Thaler, Seymour 35–36
Thomas, Clarence 80
Thompson, Frank 52
Thurmond, Strom 57, 65
Thurow, Lester 77
Times, The (magazine) 45
Tolchin, Martin 74; *New York Times* convention coordinator 10; promotion to congressional correspondent 63; photo with Governor Rockefeller *56*; photo with Mayor Lindsay and Rudy Schaefer *40*; photo with President Carter *73*; photo with President Reagan *68*; photo with Ted Kennedy *55*; photo with Walter Mondale *76*; promotion to reporter 20, 21; requesting tax returns of senators' 53–54; shop steward for Washington bureau 77–80
Tolchin, Martin and Sue 79; daughter Karen 47–48, *55*, 55–56, 84; political patronage book 36; son Charlie 46, 47, *55*, 55–56, *69*, 70, 84; writing together 36, 45–47; *see also* Goldsmith, Susan

To the Victor (Tolchin & Tolchin) 46
Toxic Shock Syndrome 22–23
Truman, Harry 8
Trump, Donald 3–4, 65, 84, 97, 106–107

Under Cover (Carlson) 4
United Auto Workers 77
United Nations 20
University of Alabama 83
University of Utah 10, 11–13, 103
U.S. Supreme Court 46

Vanden Hei, Jim 98
Veterans Administration 16
Vietnam War 7, 22, 64, 76, 109
Vogel, Kenneth 106

Wallace, George 83
Wallace, Henry A. 13
Wall Street Journal (newspaper) 3
Washington DC 49, 51–61
Washington bureau 63; collective bargaining 78; contract negotiations 79–80; Tolchin as shop steward for 77–78, 80
Washington Irving High School, Manhattan 16
Washington Post, The (newspaper) 91, 92, 96–98, 105; role in Watergate 52, 109; Trump and 3, 106

Watergate 52, 59, 109
Weiss, Ted 43
Whitaker, Matthew 3
Williams, Harrison 52
Williams, Tony 103
Wilson Center 101–102
Wolfe, Thomas 30
women journalists 27
Women's Page 21–24
Woodrow Wilson International Center for Scholars (Wilson Center) 101–102
Wooten, Jim 63, 72
World Ignited, A (Tolchin & Tolchin) 101
World's Fair 29, 30
World War II 20, 49
Worth, Mel 34
Wright, Jeremiah 66
Wright, Jim 82
Wuerker, Matt 97

Y Bulletin (newspaper) 18, 19
yellow journalism 108
Yerby, Alonzo 33, 36
Yerby, Frank 33

Zinke, Ryan 107
Zion Sid 27
Zion's Cooperative Mercantile Institution 13